THE BERKSHIRE EXPRESS;
A PERSONAL TRAIN WRECK.

Living with Someone with Alcoholism,
Drug Addiction and Abuse

Carlene Silvestris

outskirtspress
DENVER, COLORADO

Outskirts Press, Inc.
http://www.outskirtspress.com

ISBN: 978-1-4787-5562-3

Outskirts Press and the "OP" logo are trademarks belonging to Outskirts Press, Inc.
PRINTED IN THE UNITED STATES OF AMERICA

Dedication

To the late Rocky Blunt, my mentor and friend, who taught me what is was to be a better writer. I wish he were here to see this book completed.

To my son Rob, who I hope will someday forgive me for putting him through this.

And to my friends and family who saw me through this to the end.

Table of Contents

If you are struggling with a situation where you are being abused, physically, verbally, or emotionally, you don't need to allow this to happen. Don't be ashamed. You are not to blame. There is help, there is a way out. Use all of the resources available, hotlines, shelters, your church, friends, or your family. Sometimes it takes a very long time, but you can get out. Your personal safety and well-being is worth every effort.

Don't let someone convince you that you are worthless, that you have no place else to go. You are a valuable person. God created you and he doesn't create junk.

If you are with someone who is struggling through alcohol or drug addiction, remember they can only help themselves. They have to want to help themselves. Denial is a big part of drug, alcohol, and any addiction. You can only do so much for them.

Don't allow them to take you down with them because you love them.

The Berkshire Express:
The End of the Line

OUR CAR TRAVELED down the dusty dirt country road for the last time. We would have no need to make this trip again. It was our final goodbye to a place that had been our home for four years.

It was a beautiful autumn day, typical of New England. The sky was a brilliant blue. The front yard of the farm down the street was visible from a distance. It was displaying its abundant crop of pumpkins waiting for admirers to purchase them.

The leaves were now at peak with their extraordinary colors of orange, red, yellow, as well as a few remaining green. They had the appearance of an artist's pallet with the blue sky as its canvas.

My son, Rick, who had been a young teen when we first moved here, was now a grown man. He had, by his own choice, accompanied me on this excursion seated next to me in the passenger seat of my car as he had throughout his life.

As I drove down the dirt road for the last time, I looked in my rear view mirror and watched as our house disappeared in the cloud of dust. As the dust in the road settled and we came to the paved portion of the intersection a feeling of sadness and yet completion came over me. "That's it. The book is closed. That's the end of the story", I said to my son Rick. He looked at me and with a touch of sadness and yet relief he said, "Yah, I know." There was no reason to look back anymore. The time had come to only go forward.

This was not the end, but a new beginning.

The Berkshire Express:
Laid to Rest

THIS DAY, OCTOBER 16th, we had returned to gather with friends as we had ten years previously, only for a different reason this time. The first time we all gathered in the Berkshires was for our wedding. But this time it was for a memorial service for my now ex-husband, Alan, who had passed away on July 5th of this year.

Attending were friends that Alan had for numerous years. Also in attendance were his sister and nephew and my son Rick and I. For the past few weeks we attempted to coordinate this service with everyone's schedule. I had been asked if Alan ever expressed what he would like "done" when the time came. I explained to them that although I tried to talk to him on several occasions about making arrangements ahead of time he would not hear of it. The only thing he mentioned was that he wanted to be buried with his parents in Miami.

I am assuming that due to the cost of doing something like this, the fact that his funds were depleted, and because of the MS, he was not able to obtain life insurance, it had been decided between his nephew, sister and health care proxy that Alan would be cremated. Cremation is so final. Death is so final. His nephew took care of the cremation and a date was agreed upon for the memorial service, which happened to be our 10th anniversary.

When the day arrived, it was very emotional for me. I was once again returning to a place that had, for a few years, been our home. There were so many mixed feelings about what our "home" there had been. When I first began driving to the Berkshires to visit Alan there were emotions of joy and excitement, the anticipation of being with the man that I loved. Then, as time went on, throughout the marriage there were emotions of love, distrust, resentment, and animosity. But now I was going to be saying my final goodbye to him. Something that I never thought would happen. Oh, I know nothing is forever, but somehow I just thought of him as always being there.

We all met and gathered at a local state park to spread his ashes in a place that he so loved and spent many of his childhood years. It was a place he would also visit as an adult when his health allowed, where he could recall the good times, the healthy times. I believe it was times like that that kept him going. Believing that one day he would once again be that person, ignoring the reality that it was never again to be.

We all met in the parking lot and followed the rocky path through the woods down to the waterfall. This was a particularly special place for Alan. In his youth he would climb the rocks and jump into the water below and then swim behind the falls. It was now a special place for me as well. It was one of the first places that he brought me when I first began to visit him. It had been a place of happy memories.

It was so nice to see everyone once again. We all spoke briefly and then Greg, his friend and health care proxy, said "Well I guess it's time." He went to his car and returned with a black box approximately one foot high and five inches across.

This was it. This was what remained of Alan's fifty-seven years on this planet. I had never seen someone's cremation remains before and was quite surprised.

As we walked along the dirt path to the falls, the canopy of colorful leaves on the trees above us allowed the brilliant blue sky to show through. The sun was effulgent. On our right was the river swiftly rushing along with the sunlight radiating off the caps of the water, and in the distance we could hear the explosive thundering falls.

Once we reached the pool by the falls we all gathered on the rocks. For a moment we stood in silence, I think we were each recalling special moments spent there with Alan, and then each one of us had a brief story to tell about Alan's experience at the falls. This was one of the first places that he took me to when I started my journey into his life and the first time that I brought my son to meet Alan he brought him here too.

The black box with the ashes had been in Greg's care for the past few months. Greg placed the box on the ground next to the pool and opened the lid. He stopped for a moment, perhaps silently saying something in confidence to Alan, and then opened the black plastic bag that was inside. One at a time we each reached into the bag holding Alan's remains.

It was a disturbing emotion. His life that had been so vibrant at one time, was stolen from him by the MS, and ended so horribly. He was at peace now. As I believe, he was once again whole in heaven, pain free.

I had never seen actual ashes from someone that was cremated. I had heard that when they cremate they incinerate the casket as well as the corpse; so all of the ashes are not actually that person's remains. I don't know if this is true.

When I was informed of Alan's death and the cremation was decided on, I purchased a necklace urn so that I could take part of him home with me. It was strange feeling this emotion. After all he had put me through I reflected only on the good times that we had; the tender and caring person that came through at times, the person with whom I had fallen in love.

We each took a handful of his ashes. As I looked into the bag I was surprised at what I was seeing. I don't know what I expected ashes to look like. I had seen ashes from camp fires and I guess that was what I was expecting to see in the bag. I reached into the bag and I took a small amount for my urn. The ashes were denser than I expected.

It was odd feeling the ashes, holding them in my hand and realizing that this was the last time I would hold any part of Alan. I think for a moment I didn't want to let go, perhaps thinking if I held on long enough he would appear beside me.

Besides the ashes, there were several large chunks of something. At first it startled me. It was rather freaky thinking I was holding onto a piece of his bone and then I remembered it was probably part of the casket that perhaps had not completely burned. I wondered too how my son would react to this, or if he would even participate at all.

I began to pour the ashes into the small urn, which was only about two inches long and not even a quarter of an inch in diameter. I had chosen an enamel urn painted in swirls of colors. It was so fitting for my former hippy. I thought it was something that he would like.

Rick was pretty freaked out about this and said to me "Are you sure you want to do that. His ghost might be lurking around if you do." It is funny, because to this day my dog will sit and stare up at the ceiling or stare at something behind me. It makes me think Rick was probably right, it is Alan's spirit. He once called me "his angel," perhaps now he is my guardian angel.

Greg explained to everyone what I was doing with the ashes. Our group of friends gathered around me to watch. Once the urn was full, Rick looked at me for a moment with an ill look on his face. I knew he was unsure if he really wanted to reach in and touch the ashes. I also knew his feelings for Alan and knew he was hesitant about participating. Their relationship was never amicable and I told him that if he didn't want to do this he didn't have to, but in my heart I hoped he had grown to be a man who could forgive. To my delight, he reached into the bag and took out a handful and examined it, still holding them closely so they wouldn't blow away. I was ever so proud of him.

We separated into an area of our own to release them. I was not sure how this was actually done. So for a brief moment I held my hand up and let a few ashes blow off watching them being carried through the air and thinking now he would be overlooking all that he had enjoyed in his days of good health. I hoped that he was now happy.

It was a difficult time having to say goodbye to him again and this time touching him in such a different way. I wondered if somehow his spirit felt me holding him. I bent down and released the remaining ashes into the water. I stood up and watched as they rushed down the river, passing over the rocks and flowing off into the distance. That was Alan in his healthy years, his professional years, always moving, always on the go. As I stood on the shore I told him for the last time that I would always love him. Good-bye Alan my love, I'm so sorry for how this ended. I blew him a kiss and turned to walk away. That was it. He was gone, except for the small part of him that I was taking home with me.

What was particularly pleasing to me was the fact that

my son joined in. He did not have a good relationship with Alan. Rick did not understand him; he only viewed him as the enemy who had removed him from his home, family, and friends and came between him and his mother. I was proud of him for leaving that all behind him and taking the adult stand, showing respect for his step-father. Alan's friends too knew the situation between the two and they went over to Rick shaking his hand and saying kind words to him.

As we re-assembled on the rocks, Greg spoke. With the intensity of the waterfall it was very difficult to hear what he was saying. He spoke of Alan as a friend and husband and how much he loved every one of us so much and how he referred to me as "his angel."

A couple of his friends briefly spoke a few words about him, as did his sister. It was so emotional for me; I had all I could do to hold back the tears. What was in my heart was for me and Alan only to know. I was full of guilt for not fulfilling my marriage vows, "for better or worse". But the worst was not acceptable and I knew that in my heart I needed to leave in order to survive. His friends knew that as well and held no ill feelings toward me. In fact, one commented that they were all surprised that I stuck it out as long as I did. They all knew what I was getting into and no one forewarned me. Their allegiance was to him. I was only a stranger to them and now "they" wouldn't have to put up with him", as one of them said at our wedding, "Now it's your turn," were the words in a toast by one of the best men. At that time I had no idea what they meant.

It was now time to depart. We had accomplished what we had come here to do. Greg, his friend who had orchestrated this whole event, suggested that whoever wanted to join us, we would be going to "the lake" and finish spreading his ashes there. It was amazing how many ashes were left in that bag. I knew Alan was a large man, but really, that many? I had not taken into account the ashes from the casket.

It turned out it was only the five of us that went to the lake. We found a spot at the lake and parked our cars. It was extremely cold and windy there. Again we each reached into the bag and took a handful of ashes. There were a lot of ashes. We attempted foolishly to toss them into the water. The wind was blowing in our direction. It was rather humorous that they blew back at us. It was like Alan saying "I'm sticking with you guys."

We reached back in and took out the remaining ashes and set them into the water and watched as the waves tossed them about dragging them back and forth and finally they disappeared.

We drove through Alan's old neighborhood at the lake and stopped to visit old friends. We explained to them what we had done and they expressed how sorry they were that he had passed.

We all knew we would miss him. We would miss his laughter and his stories and his jokes. And even when he was an ogre it was memorable. No one could believe how he could be such a sweet caring person deep down, he had been so kind and full of life in the past, yet could be so hateful. Life had taken its toll. He would have these explosions of hatefulness and anger, mostly from the effects of MS, but underlying from the physical, emotional, and verbal abuse he had tolerated throughout his life from his father. That type of behavior was what he had learned.

But that was all behind him now. He was finally at peace.

The Berkshire Express:
A Visit to the Past

AFTER THE MEMORIAL service and before we headed home, Rick wanted to stop and visit with his ex-girlfriend, with whom he was still friends, even though it had been six years since we had moved away.

We both visited with her for a short while. During their time of dating she and I had a strained relationship. She was going through a lot at home and felt the need to take control of Rick, as she had no control over anything at home. This put a strain on our relationship. I didn't care for the way she treated my son. She would boss him around, take advantage of his kindness and his new found financial situation, as he had just turned eighteen and received his trust fund which had been established when his father was killed. Over time, as she matured, the strain released and I actually enjoyed her company.

From our visit with the ex-girlfriend we took a drive to our former house. As we drove down Route 7 into Sheffield we took notice to the changes along the way. The bridge over the Housatonic which they worked on for years was now completed. Some businesses were no longer open and some of the houses had changed appearance.

We expressed to each other the feelings we were having about our destination. It was as though there was no reason to go back there, but there seemed to be a need; a need for the finality.

We crossed the railroad tracks and entered onto Bartholomew Road. The feelings became stronger and uneasy. This was not going to be an easy thing to do, but I think we both felt that it was something that we needed to do to put closure to this.

We approached Everett Lane. It was located on a long country dirt road with the setting of mountains behind it. The house sat on two acres of land. It was a very large salt box colonial with an attached two car garage. It was a great house.

It had three bedrooms, three baths, a huge French cherry wood kitchen with a wet bar and a pantry. There was a family room, and a fabulous room along the back that ran almost the length of the house surrounded by French glass doors and beautiful gleaming hardwood floors and vaulted ceilings with two skylights, which we had used one end of this room as a dining room and the other end was a sitting area.

The deck ran along the length of the back of the house and beyond the deck was the field. The owner would grow pumpkins one season and the next season it would lay baron, letting the earth recuperate. Off to one side of the deck was the other acre of land and beyond that was one of our neighbors. The view of Mount Everett was what we saw as we would sit on the deck. It was beautiful in the fall with all of the colored leaves, in the spring with the green leaves sprouting through, and the snow on it in the winter.

As beautiful as the house was to look at, it unfortunately had a history of much unhappiness. Two previous owners had been divorced and now we were divorced. With the stress on Alan of the house, the upkeep, and the tumultuous atmosphere that we lived in and now he was dead. I felt that the house had really bad karma.

I had not been at the house very often over the previous six years. After we separated, I would drive out to visit Alan every weekend, then every other weekend, then the price of gas skyrocketed and it was every month.

One weekend I called him and told him that I just couldn't afford the gas to come out and visit. He begged me to come and said he would pay for the gas. I took him at good faith, I should have known better. Even in his declining condition he wanted to be in control. I drove out hoping I would have enough gas to get there.

I visited with him for a couple of hours and then announced it was time to go. I asked him for the gas money that he had offered and he said "I don't have any money on me." I was livid. I knew he had plenty of reserve in the bank. He was still doing it to me. He was trying to trap me into staying there. Of course we argued about it and he gave me what cash he had and off I went hoping I would be able to purchase enough gas to get home.

I believe it was at this point that I realized it was not my duty any longer to try to protect him and take care of him. When I left the marriage I gave up that responsibility. Besides years before when I was getting ready to depart this mess, I had made arrangements for him to have nurses and he had day care for the house and someone to prepare his meals. There really wasn't anything for which he needed me. We had nothing in common anymore, if we ever did at all.

Rick and I had both changed. We had both grown from this experience living in the Berkshires. We experienced a way of life that we otherwise would never have known. We both made new friends and formed a new family. We had traveled a lot and experienced so much, for better or worse.

The Berkshire Experience:
The Control Begins

I HAD WORKED all my life, as had Alan until he became ill and was unable to work a full day. He then reached a point where he wasn't even able to work a part of the day, so he stayed at home, most of his time in bed watching TV.

I would listen to his stories about how successful a salesman he was in the timeshare business. The adventures he had working at clubs in New York City and his trip to Morocco with one of his friends. He had hundreds of stories to tell. That was part of what I admired about him from the beginning. He was so knowledgeable and so experienced in so many ways. And all I knew was my home town, work, and the time in my life when I traveled the U.S.A. extensively. I thought I was fairly interesting, until I met him.

He was so proud of himself for things he had accomplished. I would listen in astonishment as to how he would deal with his customers. He would start out very friendly. He always said "Make friends with them, make them feel comfortable." Then if they resisted the sale or showed any doubt it in he would begin to put on the pressure.

He would tell me different things he would say to the

clients. For example, "Well, what is there that you are unsure about? Your wife likes it, you like it, you both said you were interested. What is there to be doubtful about?"

If that didn't work he would go into second gear. "You've seen the place. You both love it and want it. You said you can afford it. So what is the problem?" He would keep after them and after them until they signed the papers. We are talking about spending tens of thousands of dollars on a timeshare and they were pressured into it. But that was how sales people existed back then. I think perhaps things are a little different now, you can't demean someone. If you keep after them it would now be called harassment.

I could relate to this. I once had toured a timeshare on Cape Cod. I was put under the same type of pressure. I was not sure and didn't want to be pressured into something and they kept at it. Because that is what salespeople do. That is how they get the job done. It was something that I really wanted, but wasn't sure I could afford it or would use it. The sales man was very upset when I refused to sign and I left the building.

This was during the 80's. Timeshares were becoming the "the thing to do" at that time and that is when Alan was selling them out of an office in Miami and then he moved to the Berkshires and became the number one salesperson in New England.

He told me the story of how he once attempted to sell to a "couple of means" who were vacationing in the Berkshires from Miami. They hesitated and hesitated. He said he had them "right there", ready to sign. He made friends with them and took them out to eat after the tour. They were ready to sign, but didn't. They returned to Miami without signing the contract.

Alan went to his boss and told him what happened. He

was determined he was going to show everyone in the office and make this sale. He flew to Miami to their address and pursued them again. They signed. He came back waiving a check for over ten thousand dollars. And that was how he operated. And that is how he operated in getting me. He always got what he wanted.

The Berkshire Express:
The Diagnosis

WHILE HE WAS working in Miami in the timeshare business, he said he noticed one day that he was dragging his leg (I don't recall which one, I think it was the left). He said that it happened briefly and then he was fine; however, over a period of time it happened a few other times. Then there were no other occurrences.

He was 32 years old. He had lived a hard and fast life. He made over a hundred thousand a year selling and he would use it all on drugs and partying. He would brag to me about how many different drugs he had used, his experiences with them and the people he used them with. He said he had hundred dollar bills stuffed into his pockets (because he was paid in cash) and he would buy drinks for everyone and buy his drugs. He never saved any of it thinking it was never going to end. He never made me aware of the past drug use until after we were married.

He was a very handsome man, over six feet tall with a build to match, big hazel eyes and reddish-brown hair. He spoke well, he was worldly, and he had a charm that just mesmerized you.

As time went on, one day while he was at work showing a property his eyes began to fail. He had to call someone else in to finish the sale. He called his boss and by that time he had no sight at all. His boss drove him to a doctor. They examined his eyes and could not make a diagnosis. He was told it could be stress and to rest. So he took a few days off and eventually his sight returned.

Over a period of time symptoms were sporadic. Then they continued for a long period of time and his mother finally brought him to a neurologist. It was during this time they ran tests and gave him the diagnosis of Multiple Sclerosis. At that time not a lot was known about MS and the doctor told him to stay in bed. "Don't think of doing anything else, just stay in bed."

This was so difficult for him. He had been an assistant golf pro at a country club in New York. He had been a ski instructor in Great Barrington, where he taught so many people from the area and their children, as well as his friend's children, how to ski. He loved skiing. He spoke of it often, describing the sensation gliding down the slope with snow blowing back in his face and the exhilaration he felt from the whole experience. He felt freedom from everything when he skied.

This vital, energetic, handsome man did for once what he was told; for the most part he stayed in bed. There was no more golf, though he dreamed of once again being out on the course; there was no more skiing, though he spoke of it all the time to his doctors saying "I am going to ski again." Even during his most difficult times after we were married, he would tell his doctors that he was going to beat this, he was going to ski once again. They were polite to him, nodded, and said "maybe." It was enough encouragement for him to keep going.

At one point early in the disease, his walking became extremely labored and he had to use crutches. Then he was confined to a wheel chair. But he was determined that was not going to be his way of life. He struggled and would fall and would get up and try to walk again and fall some more. He told me his mother would watch him struggle and cry seeing her child in such distress. But he pushed and pushed and finally he was out of the wheel chair and was walking again. When he would tell me these stories I was in awe of what a spectacular man he was.

It was the same with the blindness. He was determined that he would see again and he swore that he willed it to happen. I believed him and thought "what a magnificent man to overcome this. He is so strong." I was not familiar enough with MS to realize that is how it worked. It would affect one part of the body for a while, then cease and later pick up on another part of the body. This is how he later explained it to me anyway.

These were the stories that he would tell me over the phone or while I visited with him. His strength and determination were part of what won me over. I thought him to be such a strong and amazing man, not like anyone I had ever known.

He eventually was able to return to work full time. That was when he moved to the Berkshires. Heat was a factor. He was told that high temperatures are not good for someone with MS and being in the heat of Miami was not helping him. The Berkshires had been his second home as a child and the family still had their summer home there, though they no longer used it. His father let him stay at the house and that was where he lived year round.

It was during this time, because it was a seasonal house with the exception of one or two other residents in the neighborhood, he was the only one there. He became bored, drank, and continued with his drugs. He would refer to himself as a "functioning alcoholic." He never missed a day of work and no one ever knew what he was doing as far as his addictions.

It was during this time that is MS started showing its affects again. He ended up moving out of the house. His father later rented it out and when his father became very ill and didn't want the bother of it any longer, he sold it to a person who had rented it for a short time.

Alan had lived at various locations throughout Great Barrington and Egremont during his working years in the Berkshires. At which time, he was also drinking and using drugs. Cocaine was his drug of choice, but he also used pot.

When he was living in New York City, during his midtwenties he told me stories of using Quaaludes and other sorts of drugs. His drug use went back to when he was nine years old and his older sister, as he told the story to me, was using pot and read to him out of a book that pot was an "herb" and it was not harmful. So at that point she got him started on it. The whole family was very dysfunctional. When they say money doesn't buy happiness, it is really is true.

But it was during his time living in Great Barrington and Egremont that he "hit bottom." He knew he couldn't continue like this and started attending AA meetings and met his sponsor. He was such a nice man, so talented at his professional craft, and he turned out to be a good friend to both of us.

It was always in the back of his mind if the drug use had anything to do with the MS developing. No one really had an answer for him, but I too often wondered if it contributed to it. Later on, during his treatments for the MS, he was again using pot and crack. I blamed myself and the stress of marriage and home ownership for his decline, but I truly believe that the illegal drugs probably had a lot to do with it too.

The Berkshire Express:
The Beginning of the Roller Coaster

DURING THE BEGINNING months of our relationship he appeared to be in good health. He was able to walk, drive, and function as a person without a disability. But he did spend ninety percent of his time in bed. I always believed that he could do more than he did, but he would say that he would get tired very quickly and who was I to doubt what he was feeling. In the beginning I just wanted to be with him and this was very acceptable, although foreign to me.

When I would visit, I would tell him stories of events that occurred in my life during the week. He seemed to humor me, but he would also get angry at times and say he didn't want to hear it. Then he would start with his stories about what he "used" to do. I realized how confined he was, but I didn't see him as disabled. I always only saw this tall handsome man. He was like any other guy, except now he was gray haired (maybe from the effects of the MS or the drugs) and he spent his time in bed.

I grew to admire him and his strength. He became a hero type figure to me for all he had been through with the MS and how it seemed he had conquered it so many times. I admired his strength to carry on through all the ordeals. I guess in a small way I even respected him for what he was dealing with and handling rather well considering.

At one point in my life, after we were married, I was missing work and the acquaintances that I would make. I wasn't used to being in the house all the time. Yes, we would go to the store together, take drives to New York or up to Tanglewood and that area, but it wasn't the same. I was the type that needed to work. I needed to feel that I was accomplishing something, making my time count for something.

He didn't want me to work. He wanted me with him. After he got his inheritance he said "People like us don't work. We stay home; enjoy our home, our life style." Yes we had a beautiful home and in the beginning a great lifestyle and we did enjoy being with each other. But I still needed something else.

Finally I was becoming agitated and cranky and I needed an outlet. I wanted to do the thing that I knew best, work.

At various times I had several wonderful part-time jobs. The first was working at the Egremont Inn. The owners knew that I was somewhat new to the area and they knew Alan, much better than I did. Alan had mentioned in conversation that I was looking for a part time job. They called me and asked if I would be interested in working for them.

I was thrilled. I always dreamed of working in an inn, if not owning one. I had no idea what was involved in it, but they gave me the opportunity to find out. They told me to come in for a week and try it out. They informed me that it was hard work and it was not for everyone.

I worked the front desk, where I met the actor; let's call him J.T. and his family. They regularly came there on vacation. That was such a thrill for me. I was a huge fan of his. There were also famous authors that vacationed there.

I worked their briefly and there was so much to concentrate on, it was difficult thinking of Alan at home alone, I was at that time very considerate of him. My concentration was blocked by him. I needed to learn all the ins and outs and scheduling times, etc. I just couldn't do it. They understood my situation and I thanked them for letting me try it out.

Then I worked at a travel agency just at the end of our street. It was a small office that provided bus trips for locals to NYC and various other locations. The office also doubled as the school bus office where records had to be kept on the buses and their use. I thought this would be a good place to work because it was so close to home and it was only a few hours a day. Every day when I would go home we would get into an argument about me working.

He was so angry that he couldn't work and I could. He wanted someone with him at home keeping him company. A working wife just wasn't going to work as far as he was concerned. His words to me were, "I didn't get married so that I would still be alone. I want you at home with me."

This frustrated me, as I had been on my own for numerous years and was not used to someone telling me what to do. My first husband was very easy going and he and I would do what we wanted apart and together. Neither one of us was interested in being involved with another person, we just enjoyed our time with our friends and family and we enjoyed even more our time together. Had I known our time together was going to be cut short I would have definitely spent more time with him and less with friends and family.

Another interesting job I had was working for a New York designer. His office was in our town, so I thought Alan would have no objection. I would be making money and I would be close to home. He could see that I truly needed this time to express my ideas and he agreed to let me go for the interview. It appeared to be a job of some prestige and I believe that is why he agreed to it.

I made the appointment for the interview and made sure I was dressed very professionally. I wore stylish dark blue top and loose fitting pants of blue, black, and rust color designs. My hair was done in a current style. When I walked in the door of the business the owner looked me over and said "I like what I see. You know how to put things together well."

I was hired for this job to "organize him." I set up his office and organized it. I began to learn about designing, textures, materials, etc. I met some very interesting people who would come in and ask him to redecorate their homes. Many of these people had homes in the City, as well as a summer home in the country. It was really a great job that I would have loved to have stayed on; however after 911 Alan asked me to quit. Everything in the country had changed after 911. We didn't know what was coming next, if we would even have another day. So he wanted me by his side at all times.

I also worked for an attorney. I enjoyed this because it was once again working with the law, as I was so familiar with having worked for the police department and having been involved extensively with real estate. I had taken several real estate courses at one time and once took the exam years before. I had purchased several houses and decorated them myself. I loved everything there was about real estate and this attorney also dealt with that, as well as criminal cases.

He was a New York lawyer now working in the Berkshires, with another office in New York. We had a small courthouse in South County and I would prepare his paper work for his cases. I also made some connections that would be valuable to me later on. However, Alan managed to come to the office one day and met the attorney. There were several in the building. He did not like the idea of so many men being around I guess. Not to mention this attorney was rather handsome.

Once again, he demanded that I quit.

My next job was as director in an elderly housing complex in Connecticut. This I really enjoyed. The people living there were so sweet. They would come into my office every day and visit with me. We got to know each other very well. They would ask for assistance in different areas and I was so pleased to help them. On Tuesday nights I would have to leave home and attend the board meeting. This did not go over well at all. He wanted his dinner come hell or high water and I wasn't to leave until he had finished his meal.

There were days that he would call the office and talk. I enjoyed it for a while, but then the conversation would turn to "Why don't you come home? You don't need to be working. I can support you." He was losing site of the reason that I wanted to work. Or he just didn't care about that any longer, or maybe never did; he wanted to make the appearance that he cared about what I wanted.

I recall one day at work I was on the telephone speaking with my former supervisor from the P.D. where I worked in my home town. We had all remained friends and I would call to keep them up to date on what was happening.

This particular day that I was talking to her I could hear Alan's cane click, click, click down the hallway. He got to my office door and lifting his cane shaking it at me said in a very loud angry voice "If you want a divorce I'll give it to you. I can't take this anymore. You're married and you are supposed to be home with your husband. I want you home now." He turned and walked back down the hall and left. All this while my ex-supervisor was on the phone and heard the whole conversation. I said to her "You see this is what I have to deal with all the time."

She suggested that I do as he asked. After all, he was my husband and that he, as well as my son, were my first responsibility. I had to think of them first before I could think about my needs and wants. I always respected her opinion, as she had taught me so much working for her. I agreed that was the thing to do. So I gave my notice. And once again, he got what he wanted in spite of my needs.

A few months after that cooled down I talked to him again about wanting to go back to work. I explained to him that it had nothing to do with him, it was me. I needed to be involved and in order for me to be a better person I had to feel like I was contributing something. Reluctantly he agreed to let me look for another part time job.

I found a job advertised in the local paper for secretary to the chief of police in the next town over. I was excited about that. It required all the experience I had had previously and really wanted to apply for it.

I went to the police department and got the application and completed it. A few days later I received a call from someone at the town hall asking if I could come in for an interview. I was thrilled. I said "sure" and told Alan all about it. He seemed to be happy for me.

The day of the interview, I arrived and at the police station. I was directed into a room with a long table and several chairs. The chief came in and introduced himself to me and explained that there would be four other people in attendance. The town manager, his secretary, the chief, and I have since forgotten who the other party was.

I was very nervous; as I had never had an interview of this

sort, and I was quiet amused that such a small town would go to such length for a part time secretarial position.

The interview went very well and I was very confident. I was able to answer all of the questions they put to me and at the end of the interview we shook hands and they said they would be in touch.

As I recall, about three days later I received a phone call from the town manager's office stating that I had been accepted for the position, was I still interested?

Absolutely I was still interested. I was to start the following Monday. My hours were 10 a.m. to 2 p.m. three days a week. That sounded perfect. So I said I would be there then.

I told Alan and he seemed very happy for me. He liked the idea of me working for the police department because, I later came to believe that, he thought it would benefit him should he "get into a jamb." Little did I know what was brewing.

Alan seemed to enjoy me working here. There were officers that he knew from town and from his former drinking days. He knew them from having a drink with them or from having dealings with them regarding situations that I was not yet privy.

I worked at this job from November to May. By May Alan was getting anxious. He was starting his nagging that he wanted me home. He kept saying that his MS was getting worse, he didn't know how much longer he would be able to travel and he wanted me home so that we could go on trips together. We had been on several cruises already and he wanted to continue doing these things while he could.

Of course that prayed on my conscious and I thought, "I can't be greedy." I knew his health had declined and on every trip we went he thought that might be his last. He may be bed ridden at any time.

So once again, I gave up my needs for his. Is that what being a wife is all about? I'm not sure. But it wasn't, at this point in my life, what I was all about. So I gave my notice to the chief. He was very disappointed and asked if I could work fewer hours if that would help. I thanked him for the offer, but told him that he just wanted me home to travel with him and that was the bottom line. I hated leaving that job. All my experience was being put aside for Alan and I knew this was where I wanted to be.

During my time working for this chief I also met a chief from another town where we had previously lived. Every time she would come into the station she would stop by my office and say "I'll hire you in a minute anytime you want to leave here." I smiled at her and said "Thanks, but I'm enjoying this very much and I wouldn't want to cause hard feelings between the chiefs." She said she understood, but should anything happen to keep her in mind.

She and I had met previously. When I first moved to South Egremont and expressed to Alan that I would like to continue working he suggested going to the police department to see if they were hiring. He so thoughtfully, I thought anyway, drove me to the station and you would think that he would have waited in the car while I went in, but no, he came in with me. I spoke to the chief at that time and asked if she needed a secretary, if she was hiring. She said "Not right now, I already have a secretary." I thanked her and left my resume with her just in case.

Shortly after I left G.B. P.D. we did travel briefly. But it was just a matter of him wanting me home. It just wasn't working for me. I felt so useless. Every time I would try to do something or say something to help him he would shoot me down. I saw no purpose for me being there all that time.

I decided I wanted to try once again to go back to work. We had done a little traveling, like he had said that he wanted, but not that extensively. The amount of travel that we did could have worked into my work schedule at G.B.P.D. But it was the control that he was after.

It was at this time that the chief from the other P.D. who was a woman, had called me asking if I would come to work for her. Alan figured it was just down the street a few miles and I believe that he thought it was a good "in" for him for his activity with which he would be getting involved. He never said that directly to me, but he insinuated it.

I told the chief that I was very interested and that I would be in to speak with her. This time I went alone. The job was again part time. I don't remember my exact schedule, but nothing that would have interfered with Alan too much. It was all work that I was familiar with. All things I had done in my home town P.D. as well as the previous P.D. job I had held.

I enjoyed working for her very much. We became friends and she was very aware of my home situation and was willing to help me if she could. I worked for her for several months, perhaps close to a year, and then it all started again. Now his activity was coming to a head and I was more afraid to leave him alone not knowing what he was going to pull next. I would come home from work and he wasn't there, or he'd just be coming home, or just going out the door. He always had some lame excuse as to why. I later learned it was during this time that he was starting his trips to Hudson, NY to get his Crack. Once again I had to quit my job.

The final job that I had there was working for a printer. Alan set this up. The owner was someone that he knew from AA. I had my own business cards and was to travel to local businesses to attempt to get their printing business. I'm not sure he really needed someone for this job, I believe he was trying to help out his old friend Alan. This didn't go well at all.

I knew it was getting time for me to think about leaving Alan. I would have loved to have remained in the Berkshires but there was no job that I was qualified for that would pay me enough to support myself. And I knew that if I stayed in the area he would be tracking me down, knocking on my door, or pulling his same old stunts of crashing into work on me. So I knew I had to quit and begin to makes plans to head back home. Hopefully I would still be able to obtain my previous position there.

I made some very nice acquaintances at all the positions that I held; memories that I will treasure forever. They all had the kibosh put on them by my husband because he wanted me at home with him. Maybe he was right. To this day I am not sure. I only know that we wanted two different life styles. He was offering me the life that I had only dreamed of all my life. And now I was finding that it wasn't what I wanted after all.

Be careful what you wish for.

The Berkshire Express:
Before it Began

I WAS A widow at the age of 33. I was five months pregnant. My husband had gone out to purchase cigarettes and died during an altercation he got involved in. I learned twenty five years later it happened while he was trying to help someone who was being attacked.

That day, my life changed in ways that I never would have expected. I was devastated by his death, but because of the way he died I became financially secure due to life insurance policies through his place of employment; his foresight to purchase mortgage insurance on our house; and civil law suits against the family of one of the people involved in his death.

I was not in a healthy state of mind, obviously. I had grown up feeling I was a lesser person than others because I did not have the "material things" they had. This became very important to me to now be able to have what I thought was "anything I wanted."

The day that I got the last of the insurance checks from my attorney I asked him to set up something for me where I would be given an allowance. I knew from previous experience that I loved to spend money. From the time of my first job, I spent my first pay check on a stereo system and it was downhill from there. He informed me that he didn't do that type of thing. But "good luck," were his words to me.

So here I was a shopaholic with hundreds of thousands of dollars in my care and no guidance. People would see me spend money like crazy and say "slow down." But no one offered to take the lead and guide me on how to save the money. So, I decided I would eventually try Mutual Funds. It was supposed to be safe. I took half of my money and put it into that. Then in the height of the 80's when it was "all about me and greed" the stock market crashed. I lost half of what I had invested.

Being in total disbelief, shock, and now mistrust for any type of investment, I took the rest of my money out and decided to invest in something solid like gold, silver, collectables.

I spent thousands of dollars on silver collections. Collectables of all sorts and antiques, I also spent money on trips for my son and I, shopping sprees for toys and clothing for him and cars and houses for myself. I remodeled my home, which was now paid for in full thanks to my late husband purchasing mortgage insurance. Because of it being paid in full and the amount of money that I now was in possession of, my attorney suggested that I either buy another piece of property or take out a small mortgage.

I then spoke with a financial advisor to invest my new found wealth and was insulted by him when he said "It's not that much money, (he was used to dealing with people with millions of dollars) but I can guide you where to invest". I was insulted. What do you mean "it's not that much?" This was a tremendous amount of money to me.

So with my immature thinking, I decided to take matters into my own hands. People would tell me to take it easy. Not spend so much. Put some in a CD. But no one actually understood that I needed someone to physically stop me from spending and take this money from me and put it someplace safe. I was so distraught losing my husband, my "knight in shining armor", and the father to my child who he would never know; advising me wasn't enough, I needed to be stopped. But no one understood how I was feeling and I was either too embarrassed for not being mature enough to know, or just could not express my feelings to anyone.

I made a lot of mistakes. I spent it all on Disney trips with my son every year staying in the best hotels. I bought my son everything possible. And found myself purchasing things I didn't even need, I just bought it because it was there, I wanted it, and I could. True confessions; do I wish now I had done things differently, more responsibly, absolutely.

I purchased houses, moved several times, purchased new cars every couple of years, took trips, bought whatever I wanted. In hindsight, I wish I could erase everything I did and start over. Now I am just the opposite. I hate spending money. I don't have much for one reason, but I also evaluate the purchase before I take the plunge. Nine out of ten times I will leave the store not making a purchase. I will walk around with an item and think about it, evaluate do I really need it or want it. It is worth giving up the hard earned money for this. Sometimes I will buy it, mostly not. I am quite a different person now from hard lessons learned and not having the ability to spend, spend, and spend. I realize now that the security of having money in the bank is much more important than the material things you may possess. Yes having nice things is wonderful, but I'll go with security every time.

The last house that I purchased before I totally went bust was in my home town. I loved this house. I had planned on building a new house but had heard so many negative stories from relatives who had built, and in talking with the builder I was finding my "dream house" was becoming less and less a dream and more and more about what was affordable. So I decided to purchase a house instead that had many of the things I was looking for in building.

I would drive around town in certain neighborhoods where I thought it would be safe and a good place for us to live. One day while driving through a neighborhood where I had had several friends in high school, I turned the corner and there it was this lovely ranch house on the curve. It set back off the road a bit and had a huge yard. I would drive by this house every couple of days and make sure the "for sale" sign was still there. First I had to sell the house I was currently in. I did not foresee that as a problem because I had a couple of people who came to me regarding their interest in purchasing it.

The deal was finally made with the sale of my house. I approached the house once again. The sign was still up so I called the number for the agent. She said "Let me call you right back. I think I can get you in there really soon."

I got the call back and made the appointment for that coming Friday after work. I was to go to my mother-in-law's house for family dinner that night, but I knew I could squeeze this in.

I got out of work that Friday and drove to the house. The real estate agent was already inside. I went and knocked on the door and she said "come in." I entered through the breezeway into the kitchen. It was small. It was similar to a galley kitchen I think. The kitchen floor was dark marble. She told me that the kitchen cabinets needed replacement. They were the older metal cabinets, but the doors had oak fronts.

I had no problem with these at all. The bathroom was a nice size and was bright with a window (not in the tub area). I liked that. The marble floor was opalescent and looked like tiny rainbows when the sun shined through the window. There were three very nice size bedrooms and the basement was finished with wall to wall carpeting. The dining room was small, but it would accommodate my furniture just fine. The living room was smaller than what I was used to, but it had a large picture window, but most of all it had a fire place. I loved having a fireplace.

I opened the front door and looked out. This is what sold me about the house. I love the way it was set back. You could see the cars as they made the curve in the road and it made the front yard look so much larger than it was and when you came around the corner it was the first house that you saw.

I called my brother-in-law, who was at his mother's house waiting for me to arrive for dinner. My son was already there. His grandmother had been taking care of him that day. I told my brother-in-law that I found "THE house" and asked if he would come and look at it. He came over immediately. He agreed it was a great house and I signed the papers, gave a deposit, and it was mine from there. A month later we moved in.

We lived in the house approximately five years. My son was at an age where he was finding his own life with his friends. Mom was not his whole life anymore. I found myself coming home from work and he would come home from school and go off with friends. He was at that age where he was becoming belligerent too.

During this time my best friend's marriage had deteriorated and she decided to move away. Her husband began drinking more heavily. Her son had a girlfriend much older than he. He was 16 and she was 25. And her lovely daughter, who was about 14, was trying her best to pull the family back together. We had all been very close. We were like family. We were always together. Then this happened. I will never understand why she decided to leave her family to this day.

It began to take its toll on her. She began acting out, spending time with the wrong people. I didn't want to see her go into the Foster Care system, as her mother had been in that situation as a child. So I offered to take her in. I couldn't afford what I had just taken on with the house, never mind another person, but I wasn't going to let her go to strangers either. She was like my daughter.

After about a year, of sending her to modeling school, trying to treat her as an equal to my son, buying her everything she needed and putting up with her "attitude" that she had developed from her strained situation with her parents, (She was now fifteen, my patience was running thin.) I knew she was beginning to take advantage of me.

One night I received a call from the police department. They reported to me that she had been found by the police in a parked car with drug paraphernalia with a much older man. They called me and asked what I wanted to do. I was employed at the police department and they were fully aware of my situation. I told them I would be right there.

I went to the station and spoke with the sergeant on duty and explained to him that where drugs were involved I did not want her in my house or around my son. He asked what I would like them to do with her. I told them I was washing my hands of the situation and they could do whatever it was they needed to do.

I left the sergeant's office and walked into lobby where she was sitting. As I walked past her I said "Good-bye" I called her by name, "Have a nice life." It broke my heart to desert her that way, but there was nothing more I could do. She needed professional assistance now. And from there she went into the Foster system.

Eventually, she ended up moving out of state where her mother was living with her family. Her mother, I understand, has a drug problem, as well as the brother, who eventually found his way out and had found God. He is doing well. She has a twelve year old son. I only pray he doesn't fall to the way side. I understand that she had a drug issue. I've seen her photos and a once very beautiful girl had turned into a very aged young woman. I learned not long ago that she had passed away from a massive heart attack at the age of 34.

I had placed myself into a very severe financial situation by taking her in. I was working to keep my house and not doing a very good job of it. Credit cards were maxed out. Collectors were calling. Utilities were in threat of being disconnected. I found myself slowing dying inside. I was feeling helpless. I kept trying to keep up appearances and it was catching up to me. My resources were drained. I didn't know where to turn and didn't want anyone to know how bad things were.

I had no outlet. I worked as much as possible to make as much money as I could. I was seeing less and less of my son, but I had to do it. He didn't understand why I was gone so much and in later years chided me for it.

The holidays were coming quickly. I did what shopping I could. I always did my best to have my son keep up with his friends who had two parents. I made sure he had the best clothes, the best toys, and the best of everything.

His uncle gave him a computer for Christmas this particular year. I was curious about it. The only experience I had with a computer was for typing documents at work. I had no idea what you could achieve with a computer. My son, Rick, taught me how to go on line. I would spend my spare time, when he wasn't using it, looking up information and exploring what this was all about. One night I discovered a dating site, something that was just beginning to come of age, online dating.

I was searching through the web sites and found one in particular. "Hmmm", I thought. "What is this"? So I clicked on it and discovered this whole world.

This was a way to meet people from all over the state. All over the word in fact, but I didn't want to go that far. I made several friends from this site, one of whom I stayed in contact with for a number of years.

But the one that really mattered was the photo I came across one night of a very handsome man standing at a marina. He appeared to be tall, well built, well dressed, reddish-brown hair and big blue or hazel eyes. I looked at him and thought, "Oh God he is out of my league." I kept on searching, but I kept coming back to this person. Something kept drawing me to him.

I decided I would send him an e-mail. I really didn't expect to hear back from him. The next day I went back on line to check out the web site again. There was a message from him. I opened the message and he said that he wanted to correspond with me. And that was the beginning of the Berkshire Express.

The Berkshire Express:
The Beginning

WE E-MAILED BACK and forth and would IM, (Instant Message). We did this for several weeks. Then one night he asked for my phone number. I explained to him that I was not completely comfortable with that, so he gave me his number. I called him and right away he said "I have Caller ID. Now I have your number".

My stomach immediately went to my throat. What had I done? I didn't know this person really and now he has my phone number. He went on to say "But if you don't want me to call you I won't. I'll wait until you are comfortable with that." I couldn't believe it. I was totally taken off guard.

Here was a gentleman, a considerate person. I was only used to dealing with the criminals in the system in which I worked and I guess I was suspicious of everyone and found it unbelievable that there was an honest male out there. He kept his word. He did not call me, I continued to call him; until one night I said it would be all right for him to call.

The first time I spoke with him on the phone there was something about his voice. I couldn't quite put a finger on it, but something kept telling me that he was in a wheel chair, or he had some type of disability. He spoke very intelligently, he was very knowledgeable. There was just something about his voice that I found disturbing.

One night after a few phone conversations he explained to me that he had MS (multiple sclerosis). I knew it. My intuition had been right all along. I just fell back in my chair. I couldn't believe this. I finally found someone worth communicating with, someone I enjoyed talking with and he has this horrible disease.

I only knew one person who had MS. I had worked in a restaurant as a teenager and into my early twenties. There was a customer who had come in and during conversation he told me that he had MS. I thought he was saying he had a mess. I chuckled a little, thinking back I felt like a fool when I realized that he had said he had MS.

He would come in on a regular basis and I watched as his decline became apparent. Some days he would be okay and others he would have difficulty speaking or handling his utensils. The last time that I saw him he had come in to eat with this very young daughter. He was shaking so badly he could hardly keep the food on the fork to get it to his mouth. When he was leaving the restaurant he could hardly walk, but held onto his daughter's hand with such love as they escorted each other to their car. Yes he was driving with his daughter in the car. That was the only time I had interacted with someone with MS.

While we were still on line, I composed myself and immediately thought "I am not going to discount this person because of this. He could be the best person in the world." So we continued to talk night after night.

During our conversations he also told me that he was a recovering alcoholic. This shot up a red flag. I had family members that were alcoholics. I knew what to expect from that and wasn't sure I wanted it to be part of my life. After all, I had my son to be concerned about, as well as myself.

He told me he had been sober for three years at that point. He explained that drinking was not a big deal with him. He didn't like the taste and he only did it to get out of his skin. He had started many years before and because of the mentally and physically abusive relationship he had with his father and the pressure from his dad to be successful and earn over a hundred thousand dollars a year or you weren't worth anything, so this was his way of coping. I took him for his word and really liked talking with him, so I said why not give him a chance; although something was still not sitting right with me.

When we talked on the phone he would tell me stories of his trips back and forth to the City. He was from New York City and his friends were there. He would travel back and forth to visit and to go to conferences of a well know speaker. He would talk about his going to certain clubs and the events that took place. I thought he was so interesting and I loved the City. At one point in my life I would take a couple of trips a year there to shop and do the tourist thing.

He asked if we could exchange photos. He e-mailed me a photo of himself. When I opened it I was so surprised. This was not the person I had seen on the dating site. It was him, but he was heavier and had gray hair. I asked him about the photo and he said the one on site his sister had posted and she had written his profile. In that photo he was this gorgeous brunette, dressed in a polo shirt. He looked so different now. I resented the fact that he had posted such an old photo. Honesty, above all, was what I believed in. I felt like I had been tricked. He explained that at the time that was the only photo she had of him. That was fine. It was a little misleading, but the inner person was the same.

I e-mailed him a photo of myself. He didn't say anything right away, but at a later point in our relationship he commented that he wasn't sure he wanted to meet me after seeing that photo. I am considered to be a pretty good looking woman. There was really nothing wrong with the photo, but he would later express to me that he used to, when he lived in New York, date woman from the a famous dance group and his former girlfriends were very rich and very beautiful. So if that was what he wanted why was he pursuing me? I later found out why.

After a couple of months of talking on the phone and mounting phone bills for each of us, we talked about finally meeting each other. We had exchanged photos on line, had conversations on line, and on the telephone. It was time to meet. He suggested that we meet for lunch at a half-way point, which would be Springfield, Ma. He was familiar with a place on Fort Street. I explained to him that as a rule, I always get lost and was not good with directions, (this was before GPS units came on scene) so if I was a little late not to worry, I would be there.

The day came when we were going to meet. I found my way to Springfield and was in the area of the restaurant but could not find it. I drove around and around and around. I was not finding it. Time was getting late. I was now almost an hour and a half late. I was ready to give up. I thought to myself "He won't be there. I certainly wouldn't be. I'd given up a long time ago." But something kept telling me not to give up. It was that same feeling that kept drawing me to his photo when I first ventured onto a new on line dating site.

I finally saw some people on the street and asked if they knew where the restaurant was located. They directed me to it. It was right around the corner. I had been there the whole time, passing it by each time I would go around the corner.

I parked my car and headed to the restaurant. As I entered, the host approached me. I told him that I was supposed to meet someone but I was very late and I was sure he was gone by now. He said, "No, he's not gone. He is still here waiting. He knew you'd be here."

The host directed me to the table where he was patiently waiting for me. As I approached, he slowly got up from his chair losing his footing and falling to the side. He caught himself and got his balance. With the MS he had sat for so long it was difficult for him stand. He leaned over and gave me a hug and handed me a long stem red rose. It was so romantic, I thought.

We sat and talked a bit and ordered lunch. I apologized for being so late and told him that I was really surprised he was still waiting. He said he was too. He said normally he wouldn't have waited so long, but something was holding him in his chair. He said it was as though "I just couldn't move". He went on to say that it was as if God was holding him in his seat saying "You wait for her." I explained to him that normally after trying to find a place for that amount of time I would have just given up. I figured that he would have left and I was just going to turn around, but something kept telling me to keep trying. I was glad that I did.

We talked for a very long time. We had a lovely lunch and now it was time to depart. We exited the restaurant and walked to our cars. With all of his talk about how well he had done financially in the time share business, I expected to see this fabulous sports car parked there. But he was driving a modest popular make sedan.

We stood on the sidewalk talking for another minute and

while looking at him I had the strongest desire to kiss him. I held off because I didn't know how he would feel about that. I certainly didn't want to come off as aggressive. We said good-bye and went our separate ways.

Later that night we spoke on the phone and talked about our meeting. We were both so happy that we had finally met and enjoyed our afternoon. I told him how I wanted to kiss him before I left and he said he felt the same way. It was as though something was drawing us together. He had deep faith in a higher power and I had deep faith in God leading us in our lives. We were both in the belief that this relationship was destiny.

The Berkshire Express:
That First Night

WE TALKED FOR weeks on the phone and on the computer. Then he invited me to come to his house for the weekend. I was a little nervous about doing this. I had never done anything as crazy as this before. But I really wanted to spend time in his environment with him. Working in the police department I knew how dangerous this could be, but something told me it would be all right. I was willing to take the chance.

During our conversations on line I had printed all of our conversations and put it into a note book. I was working at a police department with the detective bureau. The lieutenant of the detective bureau and I were good friends. One afternoon I went to his office with the notebook. I told him what I was going to do and handed it to him. I said that if I didn't return this was who to go looking for. I said it in a joking manner, but I was actually serious. It contained the name, address, phone number and any info that I had accumulated on him.

Finally, it was a Friday in March 1999. One would think an event of such importance I would remember the actual date. My car was packed. I had arranged for my son to stay at his grandmother's for the weekend and they would stop by our house to feed our Old English sheep dog.

After work that afternoon I headed off to the Berkshires. I had never been there before. I had never driven the Mass Pike before. I had never done anything so crazy before.

The first few miles on the Pike were entertaining. There was so much to see that I had not seen before. Traffic was heavy at this time on a Friday late afternoon. At the New York exit traffic was backed up a half a mile at least. Once I passed that and headed to Springfield it was a fairly easy drive. Then once I got beyond Springfield there was hardly any traffic at all. It was still light enough that I could see some scenery. I crossed the Connecticut River and began ascension that would bring me to the Berkshires.

From here out it was a long somewhat isolated drive. This was all so unfamiliar to me. There were hardly any cars on the road in this area. This was a new adventure. Throwing all caution to the wind. But this was who I was, act first, think later. A hard lesson that I would later learn needed to be corrected.

I listened to the radio. A famous radio host was on. I loved her show, romantic love songs; so fitting for this adventurous occasion. I would sing along with the songs and think of Alan. I couldn't wait to get there.

My destination was close. I came to Exit 2 on the Pike, this was it. I believed I had only a short distance to go before I arrived. I followed the directions he had given me and found my way to the center of Great Barrington. All of the businesses were closed. It was around 8:00 p.m. it figures, a country town where the sidewalks roll up very early. Not something I was used to. Where I lived the stores were everywhere and open late. But this, I thought, was "cute."

I was tired and glad to be in civilization, such as it was, after an hour and a half on the Pike. I found a public phone (I did not have a cell phone at this time, which would be later rectified) and called Alan to tell him where I was. He gave me directions and said I wasn't that far from his town.

Back in my car and off I went. This was a typical New England town I was driving through. I admired it. Even at night when everything was closed and no one was on the streets. There was no traffic so it provided me the opportunity to check it out a little.

I continued my drive up Route 23 and came to the Village of South Egremont. What a funny name, I thought. Before meeting Alan I never heard of it before. It was tiny and consisted of only a handful of businesses. It was quaint. This was a real change for me. This was the type of place I always thought I would enjoy living; unassuming, friendly, peaceful. This was a true Norman Rockwell town.

I went around the bend, there was a mountain to my left and right, I saw the sign for his street. I was finally here. I pulled into the street. His house was the first on the left. It was adorable. It reminded me of a chalet set on a hill with its wrap around deck. I quickly checked out my surroundings. There were other houses on the street, but I could not see just how many.

I got out of my car with my overnight bag and went up the steps to his wrap around deck, approached the house and knocked on the door. There was no answer. I knocked louder. Still there was no answer. I was becoming upset because I had just spoken to him minutes before. Where was he? Was this some kind of cruel joke? Was this not even his house?

Having in my mind that now I would have to make that long drive back home, I got into my car and drove to the center of South Egremont where I found a public phone. I called his number and immediately he answered. I explained that

I had been at his house knocking on the door and he didn't answer. He assured me that he was home; he was watching TV and had dosed off and didn't hear me knock. He said the door was unlocked and to just come in.

Once again I got in my car and drove up the hill around the corner to his house. I pulled in, grabbed my bag and walked up onto the deck. I approached the house, opened the door and walked into the kitchen/dining area. He called out my name and I followed his voice. He was in bed watching TV. He had previously told me that with the MS he spent most of his time in bed. I did not consider this to be a red flag at the time and overlooked it.

I approached him and gave him a kiss. He told me to get my pajamas on and come into bed to watch TV. Without giving it a second thought I did. I don't, to this day, know why I responded in such away. It was not something I would normally do; get into bed with practically a complete stranger. Though it didn't feel that way, it just felt like something I should do, it felt right. So far there was nothing about this relationship that was of my normal behavior. So I just went with it.

I had purchased a new special nightgown for this trip. It was a pink satin long sleeve button front night shirt. It had a flannel lining for the chilly Berkshire weather. I loved it. It was so comfortable and pink was my color.

I walked into the bedroom and got into bed and we watched TV, all the while I was questioning myself as to why I was so comfortable with this, it certainly was not my usual behavior. We talked for a long time and I think that night we actually made love. It had been a very long time, thirteen years to be exact, since I had been "with" a man. I was afraid I would have forgotten what to do, but it was like riding a bicycle. It was natural and came back in no time.

We woke up the next morning, showered and off we went to breakfast. There was the greatest little restaurant that had been around for years called the Café.

Alan was also friends and former business associate with the owner, Sam.

Alan had told Sam all about me and told him that I was coming in for the weekend. It was very nice meeting his friends and the breakfast was delicious. It was the first time that I had Belgian waffles with fresh fruit and whipped cream. OMG!!! To this day this is one of my favorites. I now make it on special occasions for myself.

The rest of the day we spend driving around the area seeing the sites. He told me stories of places he had lived in the area and we took a drive into upstate New York, which was just a couple of miles from South Egremont.

We had a wonderful day which ended with dinner at one of his two favorite restaurants in town, the Egremont Inn. The other was the Old Mill. We went to the Egremont Inn and sat at the bar. We ordered a delicious salad which was so huge we had to share it. Alan introduced me to the bartender, who he had known for a long time. He also introduced me to the owners of the inn who had heard all about me during his dinner visits there.

I had been so fed up with the congestion of living in a suburb and work and my personal problems, this was an escape of which I had only dreamed. For months every weekend I would pack my bag and after work each Friday I would leave for the country.

During my trips to the Berkshires, once I was in my car and passed the Springfield area where I really didn't have to concentrate on traffic, I was able to relax, listen to the music of a famous radio show. She always played romantic music and spoke with callers who were dedicating a song to a special someone in their life and would share very intimate and romantic stories about their relationships. This was so fitting, as I was heading to see "my man." I would sing along with songs that I felt pertained to us. It really passed the time. I didn't feel so lonely listening to her show. And it set the pace for my arrival to his house.

The Berkshire Express:
As Time Went On

DURING THESE FIRST months Alan would call me at work during the day. He would talk about what he had planned for the day, or who he had talked to during the day. There were also times he would say some really nasty things to me. He would accuse me of things like I not wanting to be with him because I was at work; telling me that he is the only thing I should be thinking about. I knew it didn't feel right, but I wrote it off as he was having a bad day with his MS and made light.

While deep down I knew this was not normal behavior. I had never been treated like this in my life. This was another red flag that I really should have paid attention to.

I would get off the phone and tell co-workers, my friends, about the things he was saying to me. They knew better than I that this was not something that should be going on and they were appalled at the things he was doing to me. They would tell me, "You don't deserve that type of treatment." I told them that I thought he was just having a bad day and he would be better later.

It was so early in the relationship and these flags were

beginning to pop up all over, but I always found a way to justify them. I had never been mistreated by a man and didn't realize that this was verbal abuse.

I was beginning to learn about little things that he got pleasure from, such as incense and candles and certain desserts. Each time I would visit, even though my cash flow was tight, I would bring him a little gift hoping to make him feel better and improve his mood.

As months went by he introduced me to his sister, who had come up from Miami to spend some time in the country. She came to stay at his house for a couple of weeks with her boyfriend and was there when I arrived for one of my weekends. Over time she became a good friend to me and helped me understand his behavior. She was so pleased that he finally had a girlfriend. Although in one of our first conversations he told me that he had been engaged three times. That should have been a real big red flag. He gave me some explanation and I accepted it, because I wanted to be with him.

Months passed and Alan and I became closer. He seemed to really care about me and about my son, who he had not yet met, but I had told him so many things about him. Alan had been a counselor at a school in the Berkshires for misbehaved boys. So whatever advice he had for me as far as children I assumed was worth taking. Not that my son was troubled, or misbehaved, he was a typical twelve/thirteen year old. All his teachers adored him. He was a very good student and he had many friends whose parents praised him all the time.

Each time I would visit I was finding it easier to stay there and not want to come back to the mess I was leaving behind. I had started out with only looking for social connections online, an outlet, adult conversation, and to make some friends. I was not looking for a romantic relationship but I was finding that this was a way to start over problem free. I thought.

The Berkshire Express:
The Adventures

ALAN WAS SO familiar with the Berkshires and he knew such wonderful places to go. He would take me to Tanglewood. We would bring a picnic and sit on the lawn and listen to the wonderful concerts. We once brought a group of friends with us on the Fourth of July to hear James Taylor in concert there.

There is a place known as Bartholomew's Cobble in Shef- field. It turns out later on we ended up living just up the street from there. He took me there one time while he was still able to walk and we walked through the grounds. He told me there were rock formations from the glaciers. The paths would fol- low through the rocks and into fields. It really was lovely. That is one of my fondest memories.

We would drive through New York state to visit friends he had that lived there. The country side was so beautiful and wide open; not at all what I was used to at home.

He would take me to historical homes and tour through them. He showed me where Jacobs Ladder was located and the Shakespeare Theater. There were numerous places we ex- plored and he was so interesting with his stories about each one. How could you not adore this man who had experienced so much, and I, who had been so sheltered, ate up every word.

At one point, while he was living in Egremont, somehow we got onto an ice cream kick. We both loved a certain famous brand. My favorite was Coconut Almond Fudge Chunk, and his was I think, a Banana Cream Pie. We would buy a pint each and eat it while sitting in bed watching TV.

Being a small community, sometimes the few stores there didn't carry "our" flavors and we would drive for an hour to the special ice cream store in Pittsfield. We would buy a quart each and drive home with it packed in the trunk to keep it cool. During warmer weather we would put it in a cooler in the trunk. Sometimes by the time we got home it was pretty soft and we would have to freeze it for a bit before we could really enjoy it.

There were so few things that he could do that this became an adventure for us, a challenge. It was fun. It was simple, it didn't cost much and we both enjoyed it.

I didn't realize it at the time, but this was becoming an obsession. I think it was part of his addictive personality and he was taking me right along with him. We both had gained a tremendous amount of weight at one point. That was when he decided we needed to go to a nutritionist. Then we got on the healthy eating kick and no more ice cream. It seemed it was always something.

The Berkshire Express:
The Meeting of the Males in My Life

IT WAS NOW mid spring and it was time for my son Rick to see where I was going every weekend and with whom I was spending time. He was only thirteen, a difficult enough time for a teenager. He was not in agreement with this meeting, but he had no choice. The relationship with Alan was at the point where they had to meet each other.

My son and I got in the car and headed to the country. He didn't really want to be going with me. He didn't want any change to the life we had had for the last thirteen years. All the way there I tried to point out the beauty of the area and different land marks. One of those landmarks was on the Mass Pike. It was a tree that we, from now on, referred to as the "paintbrush" tree. It was a landmark for me because I knew when I saw the tree I was getting close to my destination. As time went by it became a landmark for Rick also, it was something to look forward to seeing after a long boring ride on the highway.

We arrived at the country house. Rick was not interested in meeting Alan, but he was polite, shook hands and said hello. I'm sure he was very nervous and frightened about this. It was all very new for him. It was new for me. There had never been a man, outside of guys from work that were involved in our life. I was unsure how to handle the whole situation, but I knew I wanted to make it as comfortable as possible for him.

I went to the guest bedroom, which would be Rick's, and put down on the bed his bag with his electronic games and his clothing. We sat and talked for a bit and then we prepared to have dinner. We ate in that night. Alan cooked dinner for us on the grill out on the deck. My son wasn't much interested in eating, but not having any experience with a man in the house he didn't want to get in trouble for not eating.

That night I went into my son's room. He was watching TV. There were two twin beds, a TV and a computer in that room. He loved computers but didn't want anything to do with that one. That was the computer used to meet me and the start of all of this. I explained to Rick that I was not staying in this room with him, but I would be right in the next room watching TV. It was such a difficult thing to do, leave him in a strange place in a room by himself. To this day I feel so sorry for imposing that on my child.

The following day the three of us went to the cafe for breakfast. The owner and all of the "regulars" had all heard about my son and were very polite and sincerely were happy to meet him. They told him stories about Alan and that made Rick laugh. Alan was quite a character and had quite a history to be told.

We spent the afternoon driving through New York and then spent some time at Bash Bish Falls and Copake Lake. Alan told Rick stories of when he was a kid and would go swimming under the falls, even though it was posted "No swimming allowed." Rules did not mean anything to Alan. As he would later explain to me, the wealthy do not follow the rules.

At Copake Lake he took us to the house that had been the family's summer house when he was growing up. We visited some of the neighbors from his youth who still lived there and he told us stories of how he would take his father's boat out to the middle of the lake and drive in circles. He would go full throttle and his father would be on shore yelling at him to stop and come back. He did what he wanted and aggravated his father. He knew he would later pay for that behavior, but he felt that he just wanted to show his father that "he" wasn't the boss.

It was a nice afternoon. Alan really tried to be nice to Rick and to make him feel welcome. In hindsight, Rick probably sensed a bad vibe from him and didn't want to have anything to do with him from the beginning.

That night we left for home. Rick didn't have much to say. I knew that he hated what was happening and that he was scared that his life might be about to change.

The Berkshire Express:
Change was Coming

BY LATE SPRING Alan and I had talked about getting married. He asked me if I would consider getting married again. I said "Yes I would". I wasn't truly sure this was something that I wanted, but I was looking for a way out of my problems, and later I came to believe he was looking for a future care giver. I believe we loved each other and we truly believed that God had brought us together. I will believe that forever.

Late in May we went shopping for an engagement ring. I knew exactly what I was looking for. I wanted something that looked old; square cut setting with a diamond on each side. We shopped at a jewelry store owned by someone that Alan knew. I believe Alan knew everyone out there.

We told the jeweler what the budget was for a ring and he showed us two. One was very contemporary and the other was exactly what I wanted. There was nothing more to do but pay for it and have it sized. It was a ring from an estate sale. It was perfect. We had to wait a couple of weeks for the sizing to be done. We were both very anxious. He couldn't wait to get on his knee, propose and put that ring on my finger. I couldn't wait to open another chapter in my life and I thought escape permanently from the old life.

Finally in mid-June Alan called me to say that the ring was ready to be picked up and we would do that when I came up to see him. That weekend is just when we did that. I really was happy. I wasn't considering what this was doing to my son.

I only knew I had sacrificed for so long, that this was my time. I wanted to finally be happy and be with someone that loved me. I had not had an adult social life since my son was born. The only time I went out was once a month people from the station got together to go out to dinner. That was it. I needed someone to care for me, yes I guess take care of me, and at this point I was being selfish and was going to take the steps to do that.

That weekend we picked up the ring and he proposed just as he had planned. He called his father and sister and his friends to tell them the news. Everyone was so happy for him. The first thing his father said was that he needed to get a pre-nup. Alan refused. So his father took care of that.

Alan's father became very ill and was in hospice. Alan wanted to fly to Miami to see his father for the last time. Though they never had a close relationship I could understand that he would want closure by seeing him one last time. He asked me if I would be able to take the time off from work to fly down to Miami with him. I made the arrangements and drove to South Egremont to prepare to leave for the airport in Hartford.

We flew non-stop to Miami and headed directly to his father's condo. We would stay there until it was time to make the arrangements for his burial.

Alan had talked about the mansion his parents once had on the Intercostal Waterway in Miami and how Alan had a speed boat which had an elevator that would lift it out of the water at the dock until he was ready to use it. Upon his return from cruising around in his boat he would return to the dock, steer the boat over the elevator, get out, push a button and up it would come out of the water and stay there until his next excursion. I was pretty impressed, I had never heard of anything like that before.

Alan rented a car for us in Miami. He was in good health at this point and could drive with no more problem than usual. When we arrived at his father's condo, which was in a gated community, we approached the gate and Alan told the guard who he was and the guard let us through.

Upon pulling up in front of the building the two valet attendants approached us and opened the doors to the car greeting Alan with a "Hello Mr. Williams, nice to see you again" and they greeted me with a "hello ma'am." We exited the car and entered the building.

I was very impressed. Everything in the lobby was gold; gold lighting, gold trim furniture, gold in the wall paper. We entered the elevator door, which also was gold and the opposite door was made of a beautiful stained glass picture from top to bottom. Alan told me that it was going to enter right into his father's residence. I had seen things like this in the movies but never dreamed I would experience it in my life.

The elevator stopped and the door opened. I couldn't believe what I was seeing. We stepped into a dream. The floors were black and white marble. There were marvelous paintings done by his father hanging on the walls and fabulously thick oriental rugs on all of the floors. But the most impressive site was the windows. There were windows surrounding the whole apartment and they overlooked the bluest Atlantic Ocean and the Intercostal Waterway right below. I thought I had died and went to heaven. I wanted to live here forever.

We put our bags away, Alan called down for the car and we headed downstairs. When we went outside the car was running waiting for us. The valet opened the doors assisting us in.

We headed to the hospice. I was nervous. I didn't know what to expect. When we arrived Alan walked into his father's room. The nurse was there and said not to expect too much. He would know that we were there, but he wouldn't be able to talk.

Alan approached his father's bed. "Dad, it's me, Alan." His father looked straight ahead not acknowledging. "Hi, Dad, I brought Ashley with me." I said "Hello." Alan said, "Dad, do you know who I am?" His father reached out and held Alan's hand. It was so touching. This man who had been so hateful, mean and abusive to his family all these years was now so helpless and was now in his own way making peace with his son. We stayed only a short time.

We left the hospice and drove to a Jewish deli where we had these marvelous overstuffed sandwiches. They were like the sandwiches I had eaten at the Carnegie Deli in New York City. Later, Alan took me for a tour of Miami.

The day after our visit his father passed away. I felt so bad for the both of them; poor little rich boys. All he ever wanted was his father's acceptance. His father didn't know how to deal with situations other than yelling and screaming. He yelled and screamed at everyone, his employees, his family, and co-workers. I had been told some very unnerving stories about his behavior.

That afternoon Alan took me for a drive to South Beach. I had not been there since I was a child. It looked so different. We sat on the stairs leading to the beach.

Alan had tears in his eyes as he looked out over the ocean.

I can only imagine the thoughts going through his head. We sat for quite a while. This was fine with me. As long as I'm at the ocean I'm good with anything.

Later we found out that his father had changed his will to read that when Alan died his sister would inherit the remainder of Alan's inheritance and if she passed before Alan, then her son would get her portion. It was tied up tight. He was going to make sure I got nothing. I wasn't Jewish and I wasn't earning six figures a year, so to him I was just looking for a free ride. He had no idea that I was just the opposite of that. Yes I was looking for someone to care for me, but not the way he thought; he really didn't know me at all and never would.

For the next couple of months we planned the wedding, which we decided would be held at the Egremont Inn. We began to write our guest list. This became an issue, as it always does. We wanted to keep it small, as he was living on disability and two small incomes from trusts established by his late mother. His money that he had made from his time share earnings was long gone. Later I found out where it had all gone. He had been spending money on elaborate dinners for us and taking drives all over the county, talking it up like he still had money set aside.

We often argued about why I needed to invite my friends and co-workers and not just my family. I think he would have preferred it if I hadn't invited anyone. I didn't realize at this time that he was attempting to disconnect me from everyone back home. But I stood my ground on this one and insisted they were being invited.

Invitations were chosen. Because the single red rose had been such a part of our relationship, (every time we met he would have one for me, as well as the first time we met) I chose the invitations that were black and white with a single red rose. We both thought it was very fitting. I ordered, addressed and sent them out. Plans were coming together.

In August, Rick and I packed up everything in our house and moved it to the Berkshires. This was it. We had given away our cats, because Alan said he was allergic. It broke my heart and I knew it wasn't the right thing to do, but I was becoming financially more and more desperate. During this time my son's best friend, his cat Tango, ran away. He never forgot about that cat and I don't think he will ever forgive me for letting that happen.

My Old English sheep dog had passed away on my birthday while I was in the Berkshires visiting Alan. He was supposed to have been fed and watered by my son at home but something happened and he just died. I was very upset and yet it was a blessing in that I was not going to be able to take my dog with me because the landlord didn't want a dog there. I didn't want to give up my dog and my son's cat ran away, two things for which I have never been able to forgive myself. It turns out it was all part of Alan's control issue. He wanted all the attention and couldn't stand having to share it with anything or anyone. Had I been more alert and less desperate I would have realized this red flag.

I had given up a lot for this relationship. I left my home that I loved, gave up my pets, pulled my son and myself away from family, friends and his school, all in the name of love. All things I would always regret.

My son started school in September. Rick had made friends with a boy that lived down the street. Things seemed like they might be okay. At least he had a friend.

The first day of school my heart broke for him. He stood out at the bus stop waiting for a bus full of strangers to arrive. He was starting 8th grade. It is tough enough being a teenager without all these pressures on you too.

I worried all day if he would come back or if he would attempt to run away back home. He had done similar things like this in the past. One time I had enrolled him in a civilian police academy for young people. He went one day and hated it. It was very military. The second day he ran away from home hiding in the woods so he wouldn't have to go. I had to have the guys at the P.D. go out looking for him. When they found him they scolded him and made him aware how unfair this was to me and how dangerous it was for him.

Many years previous to that, he was in nursery school. He had separation anxiety. He hated being away from me. He was only three or four years old. It was too young to be away from his mother, but I had to work and someone had to take care of him. He was in class crying and crying and the teacher put him out in the hallway. Imagine, at that age, by himself in the hallway next to the exit door; really, what a bright decision on her part. What could possibly go wrong there?

He decided he was leaving and ran out the door. He found a man down the street, who happened to be one of the biggest drug people in town, and asked him how to get to the police department. Fortunately, and I thank God every day, this person was in the right mind to bring him across the street to a police cruiser that was parked there. The officer called the station and told them what was going on and that he was bringing him to me. I called the school and all hell broke loose.

To my delight, he did return home from school that afternoon. He found it had not been so bad. The teachers were acceptable, he had talked to some kids, and maybe it wouldn't be so bad after all. After all, he was the city kid and they all wanted to hear about what that was like.

After a few weeks he had made several friends and also

had a girlfriend, Tina. She was lovely. He brought her home one day. I went into his room and there they were sitting on his bed talking and watching TV. She came from a single parent home also. Her parents were divorced. She was beautiful, and yet her behavior was tom boyish. That was a characteristic that Rick found attractive in a girl. He always went for the strong, self-sufficient girls.

Alan had talked about the fact that we should buy a bigger house. Rick needed his space, as well as we did. So we began the search for a new home. We looked at several nice places and then one day the realtor brought us way out into the country the next town over, the house was on a private dirt road.

As we approached the house I couldn't believe my eyes. It was, to me, a mini mansion on two acres of land. Set beyond the house was the Housatonic River which was shielded by the woods and beyond that was Mt. Everett.

Alan had taken me up onto Mt. Everett during one of my visits. There was a beautiful lake there where we sat on the rocks on the water's edge and he told me stories about he and his golden retriever, Arlo, and the trips he would take up to the mountain with him and let him swim in the lake. He tried so hard to relive his past in so many ways, always to his detriment.

We pulled into the driveway of the enormous blue colonial. I couldn't believe what I was seeing. It had a lovely covered front porch and a two car garage and so much land where there could be so much beautiful landscaping done to it. I could picture fabulous flower gardens with arbors and a vegetable garden. All things I had at my house and missed so desperately.

We entered the house through the porch into this

magnificent family room. There was a very large fire place with book shelves and a cabinet on one side and door to the closet on the other side and the garage entrance next to that.

The back of the room was a beautiful wall of glass with a large glass door leading out onto a deck that over looked farmland where there was a pumpkin patch that had to be three acres. That was part of the neighbor's farm.

As we walked into the kitchen it took my breath away. It was blue tiled walls, a deep cream colored porcelain sink and on the other side of the room was a wet bar. In the middle of the kitchen floor was a freestanding Jen Air stove with a grill and griddle next to the cooking top. All the cabinets and stove were finished in cherry. We were told this was French kitchen. Aside the front door, just off the kitchen, was a huge pantry closet.

As we went through the kitchen we approached another room overlooking the back yard and the pumpkin patch. The whole back wall consisted of French doors leading onto a larger deck. The floors in this room were hard wood, where the rest of the house was wall to wall carpeting. Off of that room was a guest bathroom with the corner shower and laundry facility and next to that was the guest bedroom.

We then headed upstairs. At that time Alan was able to maneuver the stairs with no problem. I, as well as the real estate agent who had been a long-time friend of his, suggested the stairs may not be a good idea in the future when his MS gets worse. He didn't want to face that and said, "When the time comes I will manage".

The first room on the right was a bedroom with a wall of sliding closet doors, private bath with a corner glass shower, as well as a linen cabinet and a mirror over the vanity that covered almost the whole length of the wall.

Down the hall was the master bedroom. It had cathedral ceiling, a very large walk in closet with shelves for storage of shoes, lots and lots of shoes. The bedroom was enormous. Off the bedroom was the master bath. There was a glass corner shower, a whirlpool tub and a marble sink with a mirror also covering the wall the length of the vanity.

As we walked out of the bedroom onto the balcony overlooking the enormous room downstairs, above us were two skylights. The place was fabulous. We both really loved it. My concern was the money to pay for it. Alan's father had passed away and the inheritance was to be received in very large increments of $250,000 each quarter for a certain amount of time and then the remaining balance would be paid in monthly installments. He had no doubt that we could afford this.

The realtor had explained to him that the house presently belonged to a longtime acquaintance of theirs. It was in foreclosure and he was getting a divorce. This made Alan want it even more. He didn't like this guy and the fact that he was about to lose everything made Alan want to take it away from him even more. I hadn't realized how revengeful he could be. She also informed us that the first owners had been divorced.

As beautiful as the house was, I was getting a bad feeling about it. There seemed to be a lot of negative karma about this place. "Perhaps we should continue to look elsewhere", I said. He was obstinate about it.

He bought the house on that country dirt road with two acres of land and the mountain in the back ground. This was the slow beginning to a very long end.

The Berkshire Express:
The Wedding

WE HAD DECIDED on a fall wedding at the Egremont Inn. It was an exciting time. All of our friends, family, and my former co-workers were all invited. I had some mixed feelings about the marriage. I had always been so independent and after thirteen years of being on my own I was not used to "reporting" to a male my every move. But I did love him. I loved being in the Berkshires and I loved the idea of escaping the pressures I had at home.

Alan had contracted pneumonia just prior to our wedding. So besides the MS he was in bed for that. I told him people would understand it we had to postpone the wedding, but he insisted that he was going to be there. This was happening. And what Alan wants, Alan gets, one way or the other.

The morning of the wedding Alan headed to the inn with his two best men to get ready. Rick and I stayed behind at the house to prepare. I had purchased Rick a new blue suit. He looked so handsome in it. He had not been in a suit since he was very young when I used to dress him up for the holidays.

I had purchased back home a pale yellow chiffon long dress with a beaded bodes. It was very pretty. Rick and I were ready to leave for the inn. I told him that I was having second thoughts and hoped that at the point in the service when the JP would ask if anyone objected someone would say yes. And that would be it. It would be all over. We would pack our things and move back to our home.

We arrived at the inn and there was so much going on. Plants with candles that we had ordered were still being set on each table. Guests were milling around. Dishes were clanking in the kitchen. It was all rather exciting.

The owner, who was in charge of the wedding, told Rick and me to take our positions inside the inn and wait for the signal from her to begin the procession out. He was giving me away. I think he took this literally and didn't really want to be giving his mother away to anyone.

As we entered onto the front porch where the ceremony was to take place there was a jumble of people standing around talking. No organization at all. No one knew we were there until someone of the guests finally said "There's Ashley and Rick" and everyone moved aside. At this point we were already to the arbor. Our guests had missed the whole entrance of the bride and her son.

There under the white arbor, which we had decorated with white tooling and beautiful bouquets of white silk flowers, stood the JP. In front of the arbor stood Alan in his large frame, dressed in his black custom suit. Next to him stood his two best friends, his best men, yes two. On the other side of the arbor stood my former co-worker and bride's maid dressed in her dark blue evening dress.

The ceremony proceeded. The JP reached the part of the ceremony "If anyone objects to this marriage" and there was silence. No one would do it. No one would save me. My son burst into tears and cried through the rest of the ceremony.

He knew we were doomed. I think he wanted to speak up but was perhaps afraid of ramifications from Alan if he did. He never admitted this to me when I asked, but I believe that is why he cried.

I much later found out that every one of my friends, family and co-workers wanted to object, but they all thought that I was so happy they didn't want to ruin it for me. Without realizing it the captivity had started. The verbal abuse was occurring ever so slightly, I, thinking it was his personality. He made me cry every time we went for a ride with his sarcastic remarks about me and my family and my son. But I kept telling myself it was the MS and it would be okay, it was how he grew up verbally abused, he didn't mean what he was saying. I always found an excuse for it.

We had our reception. It was very lovely. The food was delightful. The inn was perfect. It was peak foliage and outside the enormous front porch was a majestic maple tree in full bright orange foliage. It was quite a site. The music was soft jazz played by a trio we had hired that played at the inn every weekend. Alan and I danced. We did have a good time and he covered up the fact that he was feeling so poorly from the pneumonia. We appeared to be happy to everyone.

During the toast by one of his best men, one of his longest and best friends said to me "He's your problem now." I laughed and thought "What an odd thing to say." I had no idea what he meant, but found out over the next few years.

One thing I will never forget at the head table, I was talking to my maid of honor and Alan said to me "Never mind talking to her you pay attention to me." I was shocked. This was my friend. I had not seen her in a couple of months and he was telling me not to talk to her. He was trying to take control of me and I didn't like it.

Please, don't tell me I can't talk to my friends. But I was so scared I obeyed. She had overheard this, but never said anything to me until years later.

The reception came to a close. It was time for everyone to leave. My co-workers were assembling at the door to say good-bye to me. I couldn't stop crying at the site of them leaving. I wanted to jump in the car with them and go home. I knew I had done the wrong thing and now I may never see them again. I wanted to cry out, " Help me, please."

We returned to the chalet. Alan returned to bed sick with the pneumonia. How he made it through the ceremony was amazing. Rick went to his room and watched TV, played his video games, and I'm sure cried some more.

I do remember that friends were gathering at a local spot for a party and wanted us to come, but Alan was sick and we couldn't go. I was a little annoyed that we weren't having a honeymoon, we couldn't go with our friends, and I was having a brat attack. I didn't like the fact that people were out celebrating and I, we, couldn't go.

The Berkshire Express:
The Move

IT WAS MID-NOVEMBER the day we moved from our adorable "chalet" into the mini mansion. This should have been an omen. The moving truck that we rented was loaded and ready to go. It would not move off the driveway. The truck had to be towed, that is right; a loaded moving van had to be towed to our new house.

Alan was not able to do much because of the MS so I took charge. I unpacked the truck, unpacked everything and in three days the house looked as though we had lived there forever. Everything was in place. It was a beautiful home and he was so pleased and proud of me for my accomplishment. I told him that I knew he didn't like confusion, it upset his MS, and so I wanted him to be settled as quickly as possible.

There was only one school in the area so Rick didn't have to change schools from Egremont to Sheffield, where the new house was located. In fact his school was not too far down the street from our house, but far enough where he took the bus. As it turned out the house down the street had three kids with whom he made friends. At the end of our street there were three more kids that he made friends with who also attended his school. And he was still friends with the boy who lived down the street from us in Egremont. Things seemed to be working out pretty well for him.

The Berkshire Express:
The Arrival of the Holiday Season

I MADE THANKSGIVING dinner for us. The three of us sat at the dining room table, which was quite a feat for Alan because he always ate his meals in bed. It was a wonderful dinner of roasted turkey, stuffing, gravy, mashed potatoes, squash and peas. Everyone ate until they couldn't fit any more food into their stomachs. I cleaned up the table and loaded the dishwasher. Then I headed upstairs to watch TV. That pretty much was our life.

MY SON WAS in his room on the computer, watching TV, or watching the wildlife out of his bedroom window. I would retreat to our room to watch TV. But I was okay with this. I was in love and I was no longer alone. My problems seemed to be a million miles away. I thought my son didn't mind being on his own, he was at that age where he didn't want to be with his mother much anyway. This was not the holiday celebration we were used to, but this was how it was going to be.

Our next family celebration was my son's 14th birthday. I made a cake for him. I took Rick's picture with his cake. He looked so sad. He was entering his teenage years, this should be a happy time for him, and he looked so sad.

I gave him his gifts and we had cake at the dinner table. I tried to keep things familiar for him, making the cake, which was something I did every year since his first birthday, and making a big deal of his birthday. Alan's family was not like this. They never made a big deal of such "unimportant occasions" (is what he was told). How sad to grow up thinking your birthday is not of importance. Mind games played on Alan by his father, which now carried over onto us.

The weeks flew by and now it was Christmas and Hanukah. This, I thought, would not be a problem. Alan was Jewish and Rick and I were Christians. With delight, I made a point of celebrating Hanukah with the menorah and had learned to cook the proper food. Alan sat at the dinner table and said his prayer in Hebrew. It seemed to be almost perfect. I loved it all. I thought it was such a good experience for Rick. Rick was impressed that Alan remembered the prayers after all these years. I think they both enjoyed the celebration. It was a new experience for Rick and for me.

As Christmas approached it was a different story. Of course we wanted a Christmas tree and Alan was objecting to that. Thank God for his aunt, who was Jewish but had married a Christian. She explained to Alan that it had to be both ways. We should be allowed to celebrate our holidays the way we allowed him to celebrate his. His attitude changed. He went Christmas tree shopping with us. He ordered a twelve foot tree. I had never had such a huge tree in my life. It was fabulous!

It turned out that this was the beginning of how my life was going to be. He would allow me something and then do the "take away"; a term that he learned as a time share salesman. He allowed us to have the Christmas tree, but he didn't

---

allow me to spend Christmas morning on the floor in front of the tree watching my son open his gifts. Now I say to myself, "he wouldn't "<u>allow</u>" me. That was how I felt. I will never permit myself to feel that way again. As my son was unwrapping his gifts I stood above on the balcony watching him, with Alan in back of me in bed yelling "Get back in here with me." I'm sure Rick felt very lonely and I felt so helpless. I wanted to scream out "Leave us alone. This is our day."

I didn't want to do anything to upset Alan and have him change his mind about celebrating Christmas with us. We did have Christmas dinner together and as soon as dinner was over he retreated to his bed.

The Christmas Eve which we were used to was a huge celebration with a very large family and Christmas day, as we were used to, consisted of people mingling all day long and now this seemed to be thing of the past. We would never have that time back again; I could only try to improve what we now had.

The Berkshire Express:
Keeping Up Appearances

ALAN HAD USED a portion of his first installment from his inheritance as a down payment for the house. He said to me that now that we had this beautiful house we couldn't drive the vehicles that we had, we needed new cars that matched the standard of the house. I was driving a convertible that was only about four years old and he was driving a sedan that was about six years old. They were in decent condition; there really was no need to change. But Alan wanted what Alan wanted. It was all about appearances.

He took it upon himself to pay off my car loan and order a new car for me. It turned out this would be another red flag. He never let me forget that he paid off my car loan. Whenever the opportunity arose, he would remind me, "I paid off your car loan and then bought you a new car." I told him again and again that I never asked him to pay off my loan, I didn't need him to and didn't want him to, but he insisted on it. I told him I didn't want a new car, it was his idea that we "needed" new cars. He didn't like to be corrected and this never went well.

His next move was that he went on line and began his search for cars for us. He decided that because we lived in the country and the snow and the dirt road in the spring that we needed all-wheel drive. He found a couple of models that he liked. He got a station wagon for himself, I don't really know why, and a sedan for me. He paid cash for mine and financed his. Again, I'm not sure why. Apparently he wasn't sure either because a few months later when he decided he had enough of his car he wanted to trade it back and by a different vehicle, that is when he found out that mine was paid for and his was financed. He was so angry. He wanted his to be paid for and mine to be financed. I believe his thinking was it was something he could hold over me. So he traded his car, paid off the loan and financed the new car. This behavior went on during the whole course of our marriage. At one point I found myself doing the same thing, trading vehicle for vehicle. In the end I got burnt.

A few months later, I was driving through Canaan, Connecticut. In the car dealership window I could not believe what I was seeing. It was a Chrysler PT Cruiser. These were new to the market and I had been reading about their development for a couple of years. All the while I would say to myself "I have to get one of those when they come out."

After I went home I told Alan about what I had seen. He must have seen how excited I was talking about it. He asked me if I wanted one. I said, "Yes, every time I would read an article on them I would tell myself someday I want one of those."

In his next breath he said, "Let's take a ride over there and look at it." So we did. We drove to the dealership and went in the showroom. He talked with the salesperson and I looked the car over, opening all the doors and compartments, I sat in in and played with all of the buttons. I put the seats down and opened the hatch. I was having a ball. I absolutely loved this car. Then he asked me "Do you want one?" Well of course I did and I said "Yes." What happened next I couldn't believe because nothing like this had ever happened to me in my life. He spoke with the salesman and asked about ordering one. He asked me what color I wanted. I wanted cherry red, with a sun roof. The salesman said because they were so new there was a limited supply and it would take several months to get it. Well with Alan, when he wanted something he wanted it NOW! So he suggested that we drive to Holyoke to a larger dealership and they maybe could assist us.

Off to Holyoke we went. As we pulled in there was a car carrier pulling in. And what was on it; a brand new silver PT Cruiser. It was the only one on the truck. So Alan asked the salesman about buying one. He explained there were none on the lot and it would take a couple of weeks to get one. This was not acceptable to Alan. He inquired about the one on the truck. It was for sale, it was just being delivered and would take a couple of days to go over and prepare it.

It wasn't cherry red and it didn't have a sun roof, but it was available NOW, or would be in a couple of days. Alan took out his credit card and told the sales man we wanted it. I had never in my life experienced anything like this before. I had no idea things like this could be accomplished.

So two days later they delivered the car to our house and took the brand new sedan that he had just bought be weeks earlier back in trade. I loved my PT Cruiser. I was the first one in the Berkshires to have one and that really pleased Alan. Everywhere we would go people would crowd around and look at it and I was so excited about it I would get out of the car and demonstrate the entire features and talk about the car in extent. At one point, Alan went to the dealer in Canaan and said "If you want to hire her as a sales person she could push these things out the door like you wouldn't believe."

Because the car didn't come with a sun roof, Alan wanted to make sure I had everything I wanted on it. So we brought it to a place and had a sunroof installed. Then I wanted wood grain and he had the wood grain decal added to it. This car was so much fun. I loved it so much. It really made me happy. It was probably one of the few times that I was truly happy there.

The Berkshire Express:
A New Millennium

THE NEW YEAR was approaching, 2000, the millennium. Our friends from New York City were coming up for the holiday. This was our first "party" in our new house. I loved parties. At my house I always had people over. I loved to cook and entertain. I never got involved in the conversation; I just enjoyed watching them enjoy themselves eating what I had created for them.

We were establishing a new tradition. Every New Year's Eve they would come up to celebrate with us and every year I would make a batch of guacamole for them. We would go out to dinner. They would have lobster. I didn't care for it so I would order something else. The biggest lobster they ever ordered cost $60.00 each. After dinner we would come home and sit around the bed, watch TV, talk and wait for midnight for the ball to drop. Ironically, they drove all the way from New York City to the Berkshires to watch the ball drop on TV.

In the morning we would go to the cafe for breakfast and by lunch time they would be on their way back to the city. It always made me feel so secluded from the rest of the world when they would leave. It made me feel so lonely. I don't think I had ever felt lonely before. I was alone as a widow, but I don't believe I ever was lonely.

The other tradition we began was them coming up for Alan's birthday in October which was at the peak foliage. We would have dinner together, usually I would cook because I loved to entertain and I loved to cook. Most people that I know say I'm pretty good at it.

These friends were not meat eaters, so I would broil salmon on swordfish on the grill outside or on our Jen Air grill inside. I would serve a large salad of choice greens, walnuts, cranberries, Wasabi peas, and whatever else I could throw in, topped with oil and vinegar or raspberry vinaigrette. Everyone always complemented me on my imaginative salads. They called them my "creations."

The next day after breakfast at the cafe we would go leaf peeping, which Alan hated because it was such a "tourist" thing to do. But our friends loved it, as did I. This was the couple I became closest to and would remain friends with them for many years.

The Berkshire Express:
Finding a Way

WHILE I SEEMED to be working my way through the community, Rick had wonderful opportunities at high school with their radio station doing maintenance work for the studio with the audio, but not only for the radio station he also wired the school PA system as well. He actually had received an award at his high school graduation for is accomplishments in this.

He had made several friends and had a few girlfriends along this part of his life. Some of those friends remained in contact with him for several years. One in particular was, at one point, a girlfriend. She, to this day, remains in touch with him via social media and e-mail.

He had a couple of jobs while we lived there. Both he hated and hated them mainly because Alan had orchestrated one of them. Alan knew that he was very shy and sheltered and wanted for him to come out of his shell. Besides he felt that someone at 15 needed to have a job. I was with him on that. That was probably the only thing we ever agreed on regarding Rick.

Alan tried to take control of Rick also. He resented the fact that I would do his laundry. He felt that he was old enough to handle that himself. I saw it as "controlling me" so that I would spend more time with him. I felt as though he was making every effort in every way to pull my son and me apart. So to keep the peace I informed Rick that he would from now on have to take care of his own laundry. I showed him how to use the machine. We were not allowed to separate colors and whites. Oh no, that would waste water. Everything went in together and we had to wash in cold water to save electricity, which probably saved a lot of the colored clothes from running onto the whites.

Alan hated that Rick would come home from school and if he wasn't with a friend he was in his room on the computer. He spent hours and hours on the computer. I felt so bad that I was not spending quality time with him. He said he didn't mind, he liked being alone. I didn't buy that. Every time I was downstairs in the kitchen Rick would come down to talk to me. Then Alan would hear us and start yelling for me to get upstairs.

His next complaint was that Rick was now 15 and he needed to get a job. He went on and on about how when he was young he had his own business, "Alan's Bagels." When his family would come up to Copake on weekends for the summer, he would take orders for bagels and the New York Times from the summer residents at Copake and deliver them to them. That was one of his first jobs.

His father always made sure he had work. If he didn't have it on his own, he was working for his father's company at the supermarkets setting up the stock and the signs, etc. He was always under pressure from his father to work, achieve, make a six figure salary or you were nothing. He didn't realize that some portions of this, his father's attitude and behavior towards him were a form of verbal and emotional abuse. He not only had to deal with that, but when his father would return from business trips there was also physical abuse. He, from what I have been told, was a very angry and hateful man. Those were qualities that Alan learned and carried them into his own relationships.

Rick, within a year of living in the Berkshires, was told by Alan that he had arranged for him to meet with the owner of the cafe where he would hire him to work. Rick was not thrilled about this, mainly because Alan was involved. He went to see the owner, Sam, and was hired. He bused tables and was paid very well for it. Shortly after, his girlfriend was also hired to waitress there. So that seemed to make it more tolerable. Rick was very shy and not very social, so in some respect Alan was right in doing this. It helped to bring him out of his shell. We were both in a shell and needed help and Alan was the one to do it.

After several months of working at the cafe, Rick was tired of that and quit. Alan insisted that he wasn't going to hang around the house. So off to a local supermarket he went, which was in the next town, actually the next state, only four miles away. He was able to ride his bike there. We were really located in an excellent area. We were four miles to Canaan Connecticut, where the supermarket was located, and five miles to New York State line.

Rick worked as a bagger for the supermarket and once again his girlfriend followed him there for work. I was seeing control issues with her also. She didn't want to let him out of her site.

The Berkshire Express:
Life was Changing

RICK WAS GROWING, maturing; he was becoming his own person. He often would amaze me with his new maturity.

The previous year he had once again accompanied me to the Berkshires for a court date that I had for my divorce. It made me feel so good that he offered to come with me for moral support. I knew then my "little boy" was growing up.

After the court appearance we took a drive to South County for what I thought was our final visit to the house to pick up some personal items which had been left there.

As we approached the majestic house which stood in the middle of the two acres, there was a pumpkin patch, not yet grown, on one side and Mt. Everett in the back ground. It was a lovely home. Every time I drove down that road looking at it I recalled the feeling that came over me the first time we saw it with the real estate agent. I remember looking at that beautiful place thinking "what are we doing? We can't afford this." But we both fell in love with it the minute we saw it and it was affordable at the time.

Alan's father was a multi-millionaire. He was a designer for stores. It didn't sound like something you'd make millions on, but there was so much more to it. He had to design the interior and exterior of the building, draw up the plans, and design the interior layout of the aisles. He had done this all over the world and had numerous awards for his accomplishments. It was a business that he started in the basement of his home in New York, with his wife supporting him in his endeavor.

Alan's father had passed away shortly before our marriage. I had spoken with him several times over the phone and met him in Miami in hospice the day before he passed away. My husband was pleased that he had made the trip to see his father and that his father had recognized him. He couldn't talk, but when he told his dad he was there he squeezed his hand and held it. They had not had a very good relationship, ever, and it meant so much for him to show this emotion towards him at this time.

My husband, his sister and her son became the benefactors of his fortune. This was how we came to purchase this house. He gave a large deposit and had taken a mortgage for the balance.

When I met Alan he was living in the village of South Egremont in a little house on a hill, which he referred to as 'the mountain'. It wasn't far from the truth. We used to drive me to the top of the 'hill' and we would sit and look out over the farmland below which was literally surrounded by mountains. It was the most spectacular view, you could look out over several states from this point, and he would say that someday he wanted to build a house up there. The only down fall was the cow farm at the bottom of the other side of the hill and when the wind was just right the scent of those girls permeated everything.

He never did get to build his house on that hill. The owner

of the land who also owned the house that he was renting would not sell the land. I loved that little house that he lived in. It reminded me a Swiss chalet. It was country enough and it was in an area with other houses leading up the hill and it had its own pond with a blue heron that used to nest there. Just beyond that was Route 23. I often think our lives would have been so much different had we kept it simple. Maybe I never would have left.

Alan wanted to buy a house big enough for the three of us and when he saw salt box colonial, so spacious and with two acres of land, he had to have it. He also wanted to impress his friends from the city who had very nice homes and very good jobs.

As it were, they only saw the house a couple of times. They were involved in their lives and had children that kept their lives full. Alan lived quite often in the past and he thought by impressing them they would want to spend more time with him as they did when they were all much younger. Their lives were fulfilled and traveling such a distance to see an old friend was no longer a priority.

So the month after we were married we moved out of our cozy little home and into the impressive home that he had purchased for us. We all had expectations about our life together, which for the most part never happened.

Right after we moved into the house he bought some new furniture, a new computer, and a new car for him and me. That was the beginning of the end. When I met him he knew how to live on a budget. He had been brought up wealthy and with the knowledge of living the good life. But he seemed to be very happy living simply and it was wonderful for me.

I had spent so many years of trying to impress every-one and keeping up with everyone. I was single parent. My husband had been killed when I was five months pregnant. But I always made sure my son had everything that everyone else had no matter what the cost. I worked a lot. I went without a lot, especially a social life. But my son's life had the appearance of a "normal" life, like every one of his friends with two parents. And that was how I wanted it to appear. It finally caught up to me in the end.

The Berkshire Express:
The Buying Addiction Begins

IT WAS PROBABLY shades of addiction coming through and I wasn't aware what was happening. We had settled into our house, things were not perfect but they were workable.

One day as Alan was reliving his past as he did on a daily basis, he was talking about his Golden Retriever, Arlo, who yes he named after Arlo Guthrie during Alan's adult hippie years. He truly missed that dog. He had given him away when his MS was beginning to flare up and he could no longer handle him.

He began talking about getting another dog. I had very mixed feeling regarding this, as my poor Old English sheep dog that I loved so dearly and treasured his friendship and companionship, had passed away one weekend, on my birthday, while I was away visiting Alan.

Although I was hesitant about it because I knew I would be the caretaker of the dog and wasn't sure that I wanted something else to take care of, I gave in. So we began the search on line and in the newspapers.

On line we found a breeder from Detroit that raised champion Golden Retrievers. Alan called and spoke with her and talked about the puppies, their lineage, like that made a difference to us, we just wanted a plain old Golden Retriever pet.

Alan decided that is what he wanted to do, order a pup from her. The payment was made, as well as shipping arrangements. Now Alan waited impatiently. He was the type that he wanted what he wanted when he wanted it regardless.

A couple of days later we were notified that the pup would be arriving at the Hartford airport. We got in the car and headed to pick up our new puppy.

When we arrived at the cargo pickup area we handed the attendant our claim ticket and he brought the crate with our new puppy. It was absolutely beautiful. It was a very light blonde, chubby little thing. Adorable as anything you could imagine. We put the crate in the car and headed home.

Several days later after bringing the dog to the vet to be checked out we found out that it was not in fact a male, she had shipped us a female. Alan was very upset. From that point on he wanted nothing to do with the dog. He wanted a male, like Arlo and that was all there was to it.

She was beautiful. I loved her. What was the difference? It was a Golden Retriever. It mattered to Alan because he let me know it was HIS dog and he wanted a male. I was to stay out of it. Okay. I was to stay out of it. But I was the one that was going to have to go through the dog training and vet trips and feeding it and cleaning up after it. I was beginning to feel that my opinion didn't matter at all. I was learning that his idea of a wife was a housekeeper, a slave, the person who had no voice, only to take his needs into consideration.

When we arrived home from the vet he got on the phone with the breeder. He was yelling and screaming at her accusing that she had tried to pull one over on him. She was refusing to take the dog back and refund the money. Alan never takes no for an answer and he threated to call his attorney. Finally after much screaming an agreement was made to send the puppy back and get his refund.

I was beginning to find out that Alan yelled and screamed and was very unreasonable with everyone. He would be unreasonable with his friends and hang up on them on the telephone. He would call his broker and ask for more money and yell and scream at him, demeaning him, until he got what he wanted. He treated his doctors the same way, wait staff in restaurants, clerks in stores, any one, everyone, he thought he was acting like a big shot, when he was acting like an ass instead.

I would try to talk to him and tell him that you shouldn't treat people like that. They are only trying to do their job. Try to be patient and understanding with them. They have others to attend to also. But no, he thought he came first above everyone. He would tell me shut up and mind my own business. This is the way you got things done.

It broke my heart the day we shipped her back. I cried as we put her crate up onto the loading dock. I hated to see her go. I had enjoyed her so much. On the way home he told me to stop my crying. "What are you, a baby"? "Is that how you deal with things, you cry all the time"? He made me madder and madder. I wanted to haul off and hit him, but I knew better, that was no way to resolve issues.

That afternoon when we arrived home we started our new search for the new puppy. We found an ad in the local paper for Gold Retriever pups, eight weeks old, raised by a young family with children. We called the number and found that they lived just the next street up, which in this location was about a quarter of a mile to a mile away. They told us how many puppies they had left and we made an appointment to go see them.

When we arrived we could see the puppies in the fenced back yard running around with the mother and father. We knocked on the door and the wife came to the door. She had long red hair and was very "country" very plain, no makeup, dressed in jeans and a peasant style shirt.

She invited us in and asked us to have a seat at the kitchen table. She called for her husband, who a short time later entered the room. We talked with them about the puppies. They told us all about the pup's parents and that they were very good with children, as they had two very small children of their own. We told them that we had two acres of land and where we lived. Alan explained that he was looking for a male puppy. They had only one remaining. It was a blonde one, which I thought was perfect. We all agreed that this would be a good fit for us to buy one.

The wife then went out in the back yard and brought the puppy in to us. He was adorable. He was a darker blonde that the female that we had returned. He had been playing in the back yard in a bed of wood chips. She held him and began to brush off the chips and handed him to us. We fell in love with him right away.

Alan said "What should we name him?" I was surprised he even asked me. I didn't have to think about it for more than a second and said "Let's call him Woody because he is covered in wood chips." Everyone laughed and Alan agreed that was a good name for him. Not realizing it at that moment, but Arlo Guthrie's father was Woody Guthrie. So now Alan once had Arlo the dog and he now would have Woody. He was happy, therefore I was happy too.

We brought Woody home and he would keep Alan so much company. Alan would tell him to get up on the bed, or pick him up and put him on the bed. He sometimes would pick him up by the arms and the dog would screech. I knew that was wrong. I had read somewhere not to pick up an animal that way because you can hurt its shoulders. I explained this to Alan and once again he told me to shut up, I didn't know what I was talking about. He had dogs all his life and he knew how to handle them.

Ya, okay, I know nothing. I am only here to keep you company, keep my mouth shut and clean up after you. Got it.............

The Berkshire Express:
Spending to No End

AFTER APPROXIMATELY A year of having Woody, Alan decided it was time for another dog to keep Woody company. The last thing I wanted was another thing to take care of, but it was his money and he insisted. So the search began.

The original breeders were not breeding dogs any longer. He found an ad in the newspaper for a place in upper New York state that had Golden Retriever puppies. He called and spoke to the owner. He made an appointment to go check out the pups. We got ready and off we went.

The farm was way out in the middle of nowhere, as is much in upstate New York. We finally arrived and it was not impressive. The mother and father dog were out in the fenced yard jumping up on the fence barking like maniacs. The pup, there was one left, was running around like crazy.

The owner came out and talked to Alan about the dog. Without any hesitation at all he paid for her, put her in the car and off we went to bring her home. She was cute. She was very different than Woody, who was very calm and happy to cuddle up with us on the bed.

We got her home and introduced her to Woody. Now we had to name her. Alan came up with the name Lucy, like Lucy in the Sky with Diamonds he said. And that was it; we now had Woody and Lucy. She was so energetic she would chase Woody around the yard, into the house through the doggie door and up the stairs both jumping up on the bed. She was crazy. As she got older, she would lay out on the front porch and bark. She was barking at nothing. There was nothing around. There were no noises, she just barked, constantly.

The buying sprees continued. He would surprise me with jewelry. He had made a trip to the jewelry store all the way in Lee, which was quite a trip for him. I truly appreciated the gesture. Then he would take me with him to the jewelry store to "buy me a present." He always wanted to buy me a present. I was flattered in the beginning and after a while I learned to dread receiving a present from him.

He had a behavior where he would give me something, tell me how much he loved me and how much I meant to him, and an hour later he would be telling me to shut up, that I didn't know what I was talking about.

One day, while reliving his past, he decided we had to have a hot tub. We went on line and he found a company that sounded reliable and their hot tubs were the best. He called and made an appointment for the sales person to come to the house.

When he arrived days later, we reviewed the literature and Alan picked out a hot tub that he liked. He knew with the MS it would be very difficult for him, but he insisted he had to have it. In his younger healthier years while living in Colorado he used to sit out in the snow storms in the hot tub and let the snow fall on his face while he was covered in soothing warm water from the tub. This is what he was reliving and this is what he wanted once again.

We had to have an electrician come and install a special plug for it. We had just had the deck rebuilt so it was sturdy enough to hold it. We used it twice together; I used a couple of times myself. Every time I would go down and use the tub to relax, he would be yelling to me from upstairs, I could hear him outside, "Come up here. I need you up here." How can you relax getting orders shot at you?

The same thing happened when we decided to have a garden. I missed the one that I had any my house and told him I would like to have a small garden. He agreed to it. He figured fresh veggies would be good for him.

We had a neighbor rototill the spot I had selected. I bought fencing for it to keep the deer and other animals out of it. I planted all sorts of veggies and maintained it the best I could between the shouting of orders to "Leave that alone and get up here." Finally I gave up. My escape to the garden was never going to work out.

I would be in the kitchen preparing a very wonderful dinner for him and if he thought I was taking too long he would be yelling for me to "Come up stairs and be with me." When I would tell him that I had to finish cooking he would ask "What is taking you so long. Get up here."

It was all about control and spending. I realize that he was uncomfortable with his health issue and he wanted so much to be "normal" again. But no matter what he did he was never going to be able to "relive" what he had. He would tell me that all the things he was doing were for me. Maybe in one part of his thinking it was, but all I could see was him doing these things to try to be something he could never be again, free from the MS.

My son at least was able to make use of the hot tub often,

with his friends, or just for his own relaxation. He would maintain the tub in exchange for the use of it.

The control even went as far as the kitchen. I would be in the kitchen cooking a special meal that he had requested. All the while he would be yelling "What is taking you so long. It shouldn't take that long. Get up here." I would finish cooking the meal and carry it upstairs on a tray to our bedroom where he ate 99% of his meals. I would set the tray on the bed for him to eat and he would take one bite and say "I'm not hungry." This was becoming regular behavior for him. He was having me spend up to four hundred dollars a week on groceries, specialty items that he "just had to have" and basically they were getting thrown away. I would eat part of mine, Rick would eat some of his, maybe, and Alan's would go in the disposal. Waste and more waste.

Then three days later after the failure of one of his plans to spend money on something else he would be on the phone making plans for a cruise, or ordering another car for me or for him. It was beginning to drive me crazy. He was so fortunate to have inherited all of this money and I had learned the hard way about blowing a fortune and I didn't want to see him repeat my mistake. I would try to tell him to take it easy on the spending and his reply was "Don't tell me what to do with MY money."

At one point he asked me what I wanted for either a birthday or Christmas gift. I said I wanted a lap top. He refused. He had a computer downstairs and said that was all we needed. We could share it. I explained to him that he didn't want me leaving the room to go use that and if I had a lap top I could stay on the bed with him and use it and it could be beneficial to both of us. He kept refusing.

One day the doorbell rang and it was the UPS truck. He

delivered a "cow" box. It was a lap top computer. Alan called and ordered it for me as a surprise. It certainly was just that. I loved that lap top. We had so much fun with it. Then at one point, even though I was using on the bed and I was with him he got angry because I was spending too much time on it. He felt I was not paying attention to him. Well while he watched the TV programs that he wanted to see and I didn't, I would use my computer. He didn't like that at all and told me that I was addicted to that thing. Maybe so, but at least it wasn't harming anyone.

I was beginning to hibernate within myself just to avoid any conflict. I would sit on the bed and watch TV with him as he wished for me to do. I would comment on something and he would tell me I didn't know what I was talking about. I knew these were all shades of the abuse he had gone through as a child and I tried to overlook it and bear with it. He had told me that his father was always demeaning him as a child.

Then he started on my son. He would say things like "He is troubled. He has no social skills. He needs therapy." There was nothing wrong with my son, other than the fact that he grew up totally opposite of Alan. He had a loving family and a peaceful household for the most part. Neither my son nor I knew how to deal with Alan.

One day we came upon a car for sale. My son was going to be getting his license. Alan tried to teach him how to drive, but Rick wanted nothing to do with being with him. So to try to bond with him Alan purchased this beautiful Oldsmobile 88, maroon, leather, all the toys on the dash. He took Rick for a ride and showed him the car and told him it was his that he had bought it for him. Rick was aware of Alan's "games" and was apprehensive about taking it from him. But he did. He drove that car for a while and when Rick got his trust fund he sold the car.

Then Alan decided he wanted to buy a boat. He was having difficulty walking never mind a boat. But he was again trying to relive his past. He found a bass boat for sale and purchased it. We kept it at the house and then he purchased a pickup truck to tow the boat. Then he sold that truck and purchased another pickup truck. He used the truck to tow the boat once.

We brought the boat to Copake Lake in New York. This was the place where his family had a summer home when he was a child and then he was given it by his father's upon his mother's request. He ended up having to sell the house because of his alcoholism. It was only a summer neighborhood, maybe one or two others stayed on for the full season. But it was isolated and he was not supposed to be alone according to the AA program.

He still had friends at the lake and visited them occasionally. He actually used one of their docks for his boat for a short time. With that boat he attempted to teach Rick to water ski. Rick went along with it. He had such a difficult time. He could not get up on the skies. There were four of us in the boat, including Alan at the helm. Alan, surprisingly, was very patient and kind with Rick. He really tried to help him ski. He wanted him to do things that he had done as a child. Now he wanted Rick to relive the youth that he once had.

It just wasn't working out. I could see Rick was almost on the verge of tears. Feeling frustrated and a failure he wanted to give up but he kept on trying. He wasn't going to let Alan say that he was a failure. Unfortunately it just didn't work out. He got up once and fell right down again. I told him to get in the boat he was getting cold and shaking. That was enough. I wanted him out of the water.

The boat now became another chore for me. I had to assist in docking it and putting the cover on and when it had to be towed out of the water I was part of that too. I don't mean to sound ungrateful. We had some wonderful things that I otherwise would not have had; it just seemed that all of the work for whatever it was came back onto me. I sound like I'm whining, I know, but it was becoming all work and no pleasure. Every time I turned around it was something else that I was in charge of. I didn't want to be in charge of anything. I just wanted to enjoy life.

It went on for our entire marriage. If it wasn't cars, it was cologne for him (I do have to say he always smelled so nice and everyone always complimented him on it), or perfume for me, jewelry for each of us, trips, leather furniture that he would never see because it was down stairs and he was upstairs. He bought a lap top computer for me and then later one for himself. He used it once and sold it to Rick's grandmother. He would buy vans, have them fully equipped for handicap use, drive it for a few weeks and say "I'm not a van kind of guy" and trade it back for something else. It was financially draining him and he didn't care.

When we lived in Egremont he began an ice cream bender. I swear, every night he would go down the street to the country store and buy a pint of ice cream and eat the whole thing. Then he got me doing it. We would drive to Pittsfield, an hour away, to the ice cream store and buy four or more quarts of ice cream, put it in a cooler in ice in the truck and drive back home. That would last about four days and then we would make the trip again. I noticed how much weight he was putting on but didn't really notice it on me until I saw a photo of us at a table on one of the cruises and I didn't even recognize myself I was so huge.

It started out all in fun and we did have a lot of good times in between the horrifying ones. He had a great personality and was a fabulous salesman. After all he sold himself to me and I didn't even know what was happening.

The Berkshire Express:
Red Flags Are Flying

I BEGAN TO learn that control was a huge issue with Alan. I should have seen the red flags all along and probably did but didn't want to acknowledge them. He didn't want me going back home to visit my family and friends.

We had been only married a few months. He couldn't stand the thought that I still owned my house in my home town. This was a connection that he resented. He insisted that I sell my house. This was the house that I loved so dearly and worked so hard to get. I used every last cent I had as a down payment on that house. We argued constantly about it. He couldn't understand that it was a good investment to have. We could rent it out and it would pay the mortgage plus we would have plenty left for savings or to put toward the mortgage on the new house.

He saw it as an excuse to run back and forth to my home town. I believe now that he was jealous, he thought I was going there to meet someone, another man. And God forbid I should stop and say hello to family. I was always timed when I went to visit.

When I would leave he would call me before I was on

the Mass Pike. "Where are you?" "How long are you going to be?" "Hurry up, I miss you." Maybe he really did. But I always felt like it was a control thing with him. He told me once after I had started working out there that he didn't like it. He said "We are married. I want you here with me. I don't want you off doing something else." I know he felt trapped with the MS it made him feel inadequate, which led to his crazy spending sprees and need to travel on cruises all the time.

I got tired of the arguing and assumed that I was his wife and he would take care of me financially for the rest of my life. So I agreed to sell the house.

I thought I was doing the right thing. I never let anyone tell me what to do. I would listen to advice, but ultimately it was my decision. But I was in a different situation now and thought it was time to learn to compromise.

Once my house was sold I paid off my debt and had some money to spare. I had also withdrawn my retirement account when I moved out there, upon his advice. I thought he knew a lot about investing and such, seeing he had made so much money over the years in time share sales. I was so wrong. He knew nothing about it.

Now that I had this extra money he wanted me to incorporate it in his bank account. I certainly knew better than that and because I wouldn't do it he told me that I was not his responsibility and I could use that money to take care of myself and my son. There was another red flag. Now it was too late to turn back. I had no home to go back to and he knew it. He had me captured and that was just what he wanted.

Six months into the marriage a very ugly truth reared its head. Drugs; I had no idea that he had been involved with drugs in his adult life. He had been upfront about the alcoholism, which he was always in touch with his sponsor and keeping clean in that area, the only mention of drugs was when he was younger. He would talk about Quaaludes and marijuana use but never mentioned real hard core drugs and he never mentioned any type of addiction. I didn't like the fact that he had dealt with it the past, but I figured he was much younger and we all do stupid things when we are young.

One day I came home from wherever I had been. I may have made a trip back home to visit my sister and he never liked it when I did that, it was always an issue. I walked into the house and called his name. He never answered. I went up to the bedroom and he wasn't there. The bathroom door was closed. I called his name and he didn't answer right away. When he did he sounded strange. His voice wasn't quite right. I asked if he was okay. In a muffled tone he said, "yes".

I was concerned and opened the bathroom door. He yelled at me "Get out, get out of here." There he stood over the sink and spread out on the sink counter was cocaine. He had his crack pipe and was about to inhale the cocaine. I was mortified. I was angry. I was devastated that this was going on in our house, with my son and me (who worked with the drug enforcement at the P.D. back home) in the house. How could he do this? I looked quickly around the counter and did not notice any crack. I just saw the lines of cocaine and the glass tube in his hand.

My head was spinning. I couldn't believe this was happening. I had typed reports about this type of thing at the P.D. and learned a little about how to deal with a user. Immediately I said to him, "Go ahead, do it. If it's "not so bad" I want to see you use it." I didn't really want to see him snort or smoke it or any of that. I was hoping that I could embarrass him enough to change his mind. He paused for a moment and I thought he was going to do it. Then he shouted at me and he told me to

"Get out". I slammed the door and went to the closet, packed a bag for my son and myself and left. I drove to the school and requested to take my son out of school. I explained to his guidance counselor what had happened and that we were going home. My son was confused and yet happy. He was going home and that was all that mattered to him.

I had no home to go to. He had made me sell the security that I had. But I did have family and I knew they would help us. I went to my former mother-in-law's. We had remained friends over the years and we were always visiting or on the phone before we had moved and I called her frequently after moving to the Berkshires. She took us in. I didn't tell her what happened. I just told her I was done with him.

The next day I called the police department where I used to work. Without any hesitation I was told I could return to work. I had only been gone for six months. I met with the chief that day. It was a Friday. He said I could start on Monday. He also said "You left in a hurry and you came back in a hurry." That stopped me in my tracks. It was true. I had given up everything for this marriage and I was walking out on it at the first sign of trouble without even trying to repair the problem.

That Monday I called the chief and told him that I appreciated him taking me back, but it had been only six months and I needed to give my marriage another try. He applauded my desire to do this and wished me luck.

Rick and I stayed at my mother-in-laws for a couple of days. The guidance department at my son's school called me and said they would have to report me if I didn't enroll him in school here or come back to the Berkshires.

That Monday, after numerous calls from Alan asking me to forgive him and come back, Rick and I headed back.

Who knows how life would have been had I stayed and

taken the back my job. I would have had all of my benefits back, my seniority, everything but my pension. That was gone and I would have to start from scratch regardless. I can only speculate and will never know for sure. I only know what the result was for returning. Something Alan would hold over me the entire time we were married.

The Berkshire Express:
The Explanation

WE WENT BACK to the country and Alan told me that it wouldn't happen again. He explained that somehow his former drug dealer had gotten his number and called him. He said "You don't understand. This drug is like a demon that just keeps calling at you until you give in." I bought the story about the drug dealer calling, but in retrospect I think he was lying to me. I think he was in touch with him all along. In looking back, I believe that he was in touch with him in Egremont. I recall him getting a suspicious call from someone one evening and I believe by the dialog it was him.

It was not the end of this type of behavior. His MS was getting worse. The stress from the house and having a family I think contributed to it. I believe the illegal drug use was a factor. I had told him from the very beginning that if I thought the whole thing was causing him stress and making him worse, I would leave. I only wanted to do what was right for him. I wanted him to be happy and have the fullest life possible. It was unfortunate that the doctor who first diagnosed him back in 1982 told him to just lie in bed and not think about doing anything again. I wish I knew who that quack was; on the other hand, back then they didn't really know a lot about MS.

Time went on and little by little the drug use increased. He found a way to purchase marijuana and as much as I hated it I accepted it because he used the excuse that it helped ease the pain of the MS. How could I deny that to him if it were true? I had no way of knowing if it were true, or just another excuse. I was learning more and more about the thinking process of an addict.

He knew I didn't want him using cocaine and he swore he would never bring it into the house again. Again he could not fight the desire. He found a connection in Hudson, New York from whom he could buy his crack and he would drive out there to make his buy and then stop somewhere on the way home to use it. He kept his promise. He never brought it into the house again. Now I just had to worry about him being out on the streets buying it, hiding somewhere using it, and wondering if he would make it home safely. In some ways this was worse. I never knew when he left if he was coming back, or where the police would find him.

Things were coming apart at the seams. I had held a couple of part-time jobs during my first couple of years there. I first worked three days a week three hours a day for the Chief of Police in Great Barrington. He didn't want me working.

When I wouldn't quit, he decided to plan trips to keep me from working. Finally I had to tell the chief that I needed to resign because Alan needed me home, he wanted to travel while he was able. It was all about control with Alan. I know it all came from his past, his father always tried to control his mother. His father was abusive to the whole family.

When I first came to Egremont I was attempting to find a job. I decided to go to the police department. He didn't seem to have an objection at that time, or he was just playing the game. When I went to apply for work Alan insisted on coming with me. I don't know why. That just didn't seem right and I know that you never take anyone with you to apply for a job.

As luck would have it I ended up working there. The was great to work with. I really enjoyed this job. I typed payroll and reports, filed, answered the phone and did a little dispatching. I found this hysterical because I was used to the dispatch calls from a big town regarding breaks, or accidents, assaults, big stuff. Here, I was dispatching the cruiser to "remove Mr. so and so's cow from such and such a street." Or "there are roosters blocking such and such road." But it was adorable and wonderful and innocent and I loved it.

The chief and I became friends. But when I finally decided it was time for me to finally make an attempt to escape from my marriage I had to quit. If I could have afforded to live in the area I would have kept the job. We stayed in touch for a couple of years; I would send her birthday cards each September. One time she wrote back "I still don't understand why you left."

Previously another job I held was part time in Connecticut working for the Housing Authority in a complex for the elderly. I loved working with these people. One day while I was on the phone talking to my former supervisor at the police department from my home town I heard Alan's cane coming down the hall. He tore into my office yelling at me that if I wanted a divorce he would give it to me. This was all new to me. Nothing like this had even been discussed. I had a witness for this, the person I was talking to on the phone. She was astonished at what was going on. She had no idea what I was going through.

Of course I left that job, trying to keep the peace and keep my marriage together. I always gave in and that was what he wanted. Had I fought for myself a little harder in everything I think things would have had a much better outcome. Maybe he would have respected me for standing up for myself.

I was working at the designers on September 11, 2001, yes 911. I remember getting the call from Alan saying that a plane had crashed into the tower. I remember having this picture in my head of a private plane crashed into the building with its tail end sticking out. Which would make no sense at all, but that was my visual from the phone call.

As we were talking, Alan said "Oh my god another plane has crashed into the other tower." That day the designer who I worked for was scheduled to drive to the City on business. When I told him what was happening he couldn't believe it. He immediately turned on the TV and made phone calls to the City.

It was shortly after this I had to quit this job. Alan kept calling me at work saying he needed me at home. Neither the designer nor I could take it anymore, so I resigned once again.

The Berkshire Express:
The Drug Use Begins

IN RETROSPECT, I think the use of marijuana was there from the beginning. Perhaps that is why he was always burning incense, but telling me that the scent relaxed him. So I fell into that and when I first began visiting him I used to stop at a specialty store and with what little money I had I would buy him some assorted incense sticks. I wanted to do something special for him.

I remember one night after I had been staying there for a while he got a phone call from someone that he appeared to be surprised to hear from, or he just didn't want to hear from him in my presence.

He spoke briefly to the person and when he hung up he told me that it was his former pot dealer. He said to me "I don't know how he got my number. I haven't heard from him since I lived in Copake." I believed him. I trusted him. I thought.

He never used pot in front of me in the "chalet", but once we moved and things began to change he had reconnected with one of his old friends, due to my finding them on the computer. One came from the Boston area one day to visit Alan. They hadn't been in touch in years.

They talked and visited for several hours. They were recalling their days when they used to get stoned together. His friend told him that he had a connection in Boston and he would hook him up with him. Alan explained that he wouldn't be able to drive that distance to make a pickup and his friend explained that it wouldn't be worth it for the dealer to come all the way out there for one delivery. But Alan took the phone number and one day he decided to make the call as he was having no luck making any connections in our area.

A location was set up between the dealer and Alan for the pickup. We had to drive two hours to do this. This really hurt me and irritated me because it was always an issue if I wanted to drive two hours to see my family, but this was for Alan so it was not a problem. Besides, he was dragging me along with him. I didn't like this at all. I wanted no part of drugs of any kind, legal or illegal.

We met the dealer in a parking lot several towns from Boston. He had numerous plastic baggies of all sorts of pot. I had never seen anything like this, not even at the P.D. from drug busts.

Alan made his selection, with the recommendation of the dealer. Money was exchanged and we started back home. I was so angry that I couldn't take an hour to visit with the people that I loved while we were right in the area.

When we arrived home and he got in bed and settled in he wanted me to "clean the pot" for him. He had me take a strainer and rub the pot inside to take out the seeds. He said he did not want any seeds in what he was smoking. What did I know? I only knew I resented having to do this. I wanted no part of his use of the drug, it being in my home, or me having to touch it. Now he informed me that he wanted me to roll it for him. I hadn't rolled a cigarette of any kind since I was a teenager. Back then some cigarette company sold a rolling machine with papers and their tobacco. It was a big drug era and not being one of the "cool" people that used it, I wanted to make the appearance that I did to fit in. So I got one of these machines and used to talk about it all the time as though I was rolling pot.

I attempted to do this for him because, as he explained it to me, using the pot helped with his pain relief. In retrospect, maybe I was the pain of which he was trying to be relieved. We were so different.

This was not being accomplished very well, so he decided there was a store in New York that we had to visit that sold "paraphernalia." So the next day that was to be our excursion for the day. He informed me that this drive to pick up his pot totally drained him and he would not be able to make that trip again. I was delighted. But little did I know what he had planned.

A couple of weeks later he made his phone call to the dealer in Boston. He told him he wanted the same thing and asked the price. Three hundred dollars he was told. He had given him a break previously because of the friend that had set this up and he wanted him to try it and see if he liked it. It seemed steep to me for pot, but it was, what I thought, a large amount of pot.

Alan informed the dealer, before asking me, that I would be making the pickup. I sat there with my mouth wide open. I couldn't believe he was doing this. When he got off the phone I told him that I was not going to do this and wanted no part of it. He told me that I was his wife and that it was my duty to do whatever he told me to do. Really? All my life no one has told me what to do and I was not about to do "this" for him.

When he put his salesman pressure on me I just couldn't

take it anymore. The arguing was over yes I was going, no I wasn't going. So I got in my car and off I went. I drove for an hour and a half right passed my family and friends, not stopping and went to the pickup spot. The deal was made and I left. I headed back home a nervous wreck. Feeling so guilty I thought that everyone that passed me knew what I had in the car. I drove right passed my family and friends again and went straight home.

That afternoon we headed to New York and he got is pipe for his pot. I had no idea that this was going to be the beginning of something even bigger.

I made this trip to do his pickup about three times. On that last trip the dealer got in the car and talked to me about Alan and we talked about the pot. We made the deal and he leaned over and gave me a kiss. Who the hell did he think he was anyway?

I drove home and told Alan what happened and said, "I am never doing this again. If you want the pot so badly you go and get it". He said he couldn't make the trip because of the MS and I needed to do it. He tried to strong arm me again and I stood my ground. I told him if he had to do this to find someone locally. And that was how it went. He did find someone in the area and the pot smoking continued.

The Berkshire Express:
Ocean Bound

WE WERE NOW a few years into the marriage. It wasn't all bad. Alan took me on numerous cruises. He said he was doing it for me. I say he was doing it for himself. We always had a cabin with a balcony. We stayed inside the cabin and very rarely I was allowed to leave the ship when we were in port. We did have a great time eating. We had all types of meals delivered to the room. He figured they were already paid for so he would order two entrees, three desserts, anything of which he could possibly think up.

On one of our trips we invited a friend of his and his lady friend. It was nice having someone else along. Alan did leave the cabin a little more on this trip. We would sit on the deck and have soft serve ice cream and talk with his friends. One time when we were in port at St. Marteen he asked his friends to let me tag along with them.

I was delighted to finally get off the ship and do something that people normally do on a cruise. But I wished that he could come along. What was the sense of cruising with your husband if he is not going share the experience with you? Never the less, I was happy to be off the ship and doing something.

We had a delightful lunch in a quaint little restaurant. I even got to have a drink; an adult alcoholic beverage. That was unheard of in our house or when we went out. Alan couldn't drink, had no desire to and preferred people with him didn't. I once ordered a drink at dinner because he said it was okay and then all he did was complain about how much it cost. But if he was still drinking it would have been okay and it probably would have been drinks all around.

The final cruise that we went on, I had invited my sister and her husband. Alan didn't know that I had invited them and paid for their trip. I was able to keep it under wraps until we got on board. I mentioned to him that they had talked about joining us, but didn't know if they would be able to. He expected that that would never happen and I think preferred that it never happen.

To his surprise and my delight, when we went to the dining room that first night, as we approached the entry I could see our table and there sat my sister and her husband. I made like I was really surprised. "Alan, look, I don't believe it. They made it." He said, "What are you talking about?" I replied, "It's my sister and her husband. They made it on the cruise after all."

We walked to the table and he seemed delighted to see them. Although, not forgetting, he was a salesman and he could make anyone believe anything. We sat and had a delightful dinner. Every once in a while my sister's and my eyes would connect and we would share a little grin knowing what we had pulled off.

The ship left from Miami and cruised to Jamaica and the Grand Cayman Islands. It was so nice having them along. But once again he would not leave the cabin and he didn't want me to leave either, other than for meals.

I remember calling my sister's cabin one evening saying I was sneaking out and would meet them on deck. I told Alan that I was going to get some ice cream for him and was going to do a little shopping and I would be back. Part of that escape was allegedly for him, so it was acceptable. That was one of the few times I got to spend time on ship alone with them. Thankfully we all did have our meals together in the dining rooms.

When we docked in Jamaica we all got off the ship. Alan was driving his scooter at that time because he was unable to walk any distance. As we exited the ship he told us to have a good time, he was going to go and do his own thing. So many times he lived in the past so unaware that things were no longer the way they used to be, nor was he the person he used to be. It was not safe for him to be alone, but he refused to listen.

We went off shopping and we had a wonderful afternoon. Alan went his way. As we returned to the ship several hours later there he was on his scooter heading toward us with this mischievous look on his face. He said "I got arrested." "What!! If you got arrested how can you be here and why did you "get arrested"?

He explained ever so proudly that he had gotten himself a cab. The cab driver put his scooter in the trunk and Alan asked him if he knew where he could buy weed. The cab driver said he did and off they went. He was so stupid. He could have been robbed, beaten, or even killed. It was like dealing with a child so many times.

He told us that when he got back from his "buy" he got back on his scooter and headed towards the ship. As he was attempting to get back on the ship they pulled him aside and asked him about the weed. He figured the cab driver must have been associated with the cruise line somehow and ratted him out. They confiscated the weed and they were going to have the local police lock him up. He said that someone who worked on the ship said they knew him and he was okay, to let him go. How dare he put us all in jeopardy. The mind of a druggie; I was getting such an education.

The Berkshire Express:
The Adventure Continues

AS HIS PAIN worsened he would find all type of excuses to get narcotics from his doctors. When they finally caught on and would not give him such high does, he got furious. One time in particular while I was working at the Great Barrington Police Department he asked me to alter one of his scripts. "Are you out of your mind" I said. I knew from working at the PD at home that this was real trouble. I wasn't going to jail for anyone. He said I was his wife and I needed to do this to help him. I refused.

He altered the script, drove us to the pharmacy and handed it in. The pharmacist knew right away that it had been altered. She called the doctor to verify. Now we had done business at this pharmacy for quite a while. I did my every day shopping there and the employees of the store knew me and him.

The pharmacist approached him and said "This has been altered." He made like he didn't know what she was talking about. She was wise to him and said "I am not going to fill this and the doctor does not want you as her patient any longer. In fact, we don't want you to come in here anymore." I was so embarrassed and ashamed of him for doing this and dragging me into it. I was so afraid she was going to call the police and we would both go to jail.

We didn't get arrested, but I did check the police log one day at work and found that she had called it in. Our names were not mentioned, but the call was there. I just wanted to die of embarrassment.

He would lie constantly to his doctors about his need for the pain medication. I was watching him transform back into an addict and I couldn't stop him. I spoke with his doctor and his AA sponsor, they both told me that he had to hit rock bottom before anything could be done and he would have to want to get help himself.

My world was coming apart at the seams.

Berkshire Express:
The Final Straw

WHAT WAS THE final straw? We had taken several trips to Hawaii. I was so fortunate that he was financially able to do this for us. On one of our trips he rented a car and we drove from Honolulu around the whole island. We stopped at a beach on the northern side. It was December and there Van, the skateboard shoe company, was sponsoring a surfing competition. We stopped and watched for a while. The surf was not very good. I believe the called it milky.

We headed on our way and found a wonderful little roadside stand where a man was selling pineapples. He would peel them with his machete and cut them up putting the pieces into zip lock bags. We would eat the pieces as we drove along. They were so fresh and dripping with pineapple juice.

Further down the road was another stand where they were selling coconut drinks. We stopped to check it out. Again the man had a machete. He would slice the top of the coconut off and put a straw into it and you would drink the fresh coconut milk right from it. It was so good, so fresh, and cold. He kept them stored in a cooler next to his stand. This was so much fun. It was something unexpected and so delightful.

On another day we took another road trip. We came across a roadside stand slightly off the road actually. It was a small trailer all decorated with flowers and large signs all the way up to it advertising shrimp. Alan loved shrimp. I was not a fan of it, but he enjoyed it tremendously. People were lined up to order it. They also offered a fish called Mahi Mahi. That was where I learned about that fish and enjoyed the way they prepared it. We went to this stand a few of times during our stay and each time he would order the enormous shrimp and I would order the Mahi Mahi. It truly is one of my fondest memories of all of the trips that we had taken.

On our final trip to Hawaii in 2003, we had spent a week in Honolulu and we were flying to Maui to spend our second week. I told him not to carry a large amount of cash with him, to only carry his cards and a small amount that was needed for tips. Of course why would he listen to me? I was, as he would always put it, "stupid and didn't know what I was talking about". I had only worked in the P.D. for numerous years and dealt with these types of situations all the time, but I was stupid and didn't know what I was talking about.

Well he lost his wallet during a security search at the airport from Honolulu to Maui. At the airport in Oahu standard security procedure was that we had to take out our possessions from our pockets and put them in the basket at the security check point, this included wallets.

I always hated this process in any airport. There travel your belongings along a conveyor belt while you are being scanned with an electrical device and anyone could walk off with your personal items.

Someone took advantage of a handicap person and walked off with his wallet. It contained all of his credit cards and fifteen hundred dollars in cash. We reported it to the police. The police came and took a report, but nothing was ever found.

When we arrived at the hotel in Maui I called the credit card companies and reported the theft. We had cash wired to us and they immediately sent us new cards. After this happening he didn't want to leave the hotel. He was so depressed. I had told him not to carry that much cash but he wanted to be the big shot and see where it got him.

We spent a few days in Maui. It was a fabulous hotel. The view was exquisite. He wouldn't leave the room. I had to explore by myself. At least I got to do that. The grounds were covered in beautiful flowers of all colors and palms so tall and wide they looked like giant fans. The ocean was such a deep blue. I had never seen a blue this color before and jutting up throughout the ocean were smaller islands.

I finally got him to leave the room and we took a drive to a diner, Peggy Sue's. This is the first time I have thought of that diner since then. It was reminiscent of the fifties. We had a very nice meal and got into the car, drove a short distance and back to the hotel. He was still very upset about what had happened and announced he just wanted to go home. Home as in the Berkshires, not back to Oahu. Thirteen hours of flying home.

A couple of days later we left Maui and headed back to Oahu. We had a condo that we rented each time we stayed in Honolulu. It was a place that I will always love and remember fondly.

Once we got back to Honolulu the MS really reared its ugly head. I believe that all of the turmoil from the extra flights back and forth to Maui, the loss of his wallet and the upset from it was causing a neurological problem.

Alan was falling constantly. I would have to tie bed sheets together and knot them so he could hold on and I could drag him across the floor and try to get his very large body back into the bed. Alan was six feet tall and very close to three hundred pounds if not over. This went on for several days. He finally got so bad that we had to take him to the hospital. He fought it all the way, but I had called his doctor back home and told him what was happening and he said he needed to be hospitalized.

I called the front desk and told them what was happening and that we needed an ambulance. The fire department was right next door and they were there immediately. Because he was so large they had a very difficult time getting him on the stretcher. After a short while they succeeded and off we went.

While we were riding in the ambulance we passed a parade. I don't recall any longer what the celebration was. The EMT had told us. It was an annual thing that they did. I so wished that we had known about it earlier in the week when he was a little better and we could have gone to the festivities.

Alan was a wreck at the fact that they were admitting him to the hospital. He had never stayed over-night in a hospital before and was like a child he was so frightened. I had to stay in the hospital room over- night with him. It didn't make sense to me, but I humored him as a good wife would.

He was sent back to the hotel after a day or two, as there was nothing they could do for him. They didn't know how to deal with MS. Again and again he would fall and again and again I would struggle to drag him across the floor and into the bed.

As difficult as it was I didn't mind doing it. He was in distress and I needed, wanted, to help him. I would have done anything for him as far as the MS, and eventually did things I never thought I would have to do. This went on for three months. Anyone would dream of being in Hawaii for three months, but not under these circumstances.

He had made friends with one of the staff who liked using weed. He would hire him to go purchase it for him. This was when I started leaving the hotel and going shopping. I bought everything I could get my hands on. I was so angry at him. Did he have to bring his drug use here to paradise?

It was getting close to my son's birthday. We had left in early September on our trip and it was late November. We had been here all of September, all of October and almost all of November. Every time I would call my son he would ask "Mom, when are you coming home"? I felt so bad for him. He was a teenager, but he was still so young. He needed guidance, he needed home cooked meals, and he needed his mother. I insisted, and who would ever insist on leaving Hawaii, that we had to go home.

Alan was not up to traveling on such a long flight. I think he was truly afraid because of his condition. We attempted all sorts of avenues to get him home. We called for private flights, cruise lines, anything that we could come up with, but it was all so expensive and we had spent so much money staying at the hotel for three months already. Finally, after three weeks, he bit the bullet and said "Let's just book a flight and get out of here".

So I packed up all that I had accumulated during our stay. I had actually purchased a very oversized suitcase on wheels, duffle bag style, to take home everything I had purchased and all of his medical equipment we had accumulated and off we went to the airport.

We arrived and boarded our flight. Because he had a physical disability we were allowed to sit in the first seats of coach where there is more leg room and it was right next to the bathroom.

During the flight and thankfully close to our arrival in Hartford airport, he went to the restroom and while inside that tiny little room his legs gave out and he was now wedged between the toilet and the wall. He had been in there quite a while and I was getting nervous. I approached the flight attendant and explained the situation.

He went and knocked on the door. Alan responded and said that he was stuck. The flight attendant had to assist me in getting into the bathroom. I couldn't get him up to get him out.

Finally a very nice gentleman, I believe to this day he was an air marshal, assisted in getting him up off the floor and back to his seat. I felt so bad for him, he was so sick and he was so embarrassed and angry that this that happened to him.

He had tried so hard to do things that the average person would do, things that he used to do, and every time he tried he ended up in a predicament. My heart broke for him every time he had difficulty. I wanted to make him "all better" and I knew that was impossible. All he wanted was to be "normal" again and with the MS that would never happen.

When we got home things didn't improve. His health only deteriorated more and more. He was falling more and more and I was dragging him across the floor either by his arms or by a sheet tied in knots for him to hold onto. Then between the two of us we struggled to get him into bed. On a couple of occasions I had to get my son involved because I alone just could not get him up. He was becoming more and more frustrated. He was embarrassed that this was happening to him. He hated himself for being sick and it was being taken out on anyone near him.

I once told him that the MS was not a problem with me. I would do all I could to help him, it wasn't his fault that he was sick and I didn't mind dragging him across the floor, lifting him up, changing sheets in the middle of the night because he had an "accident" it was all part of it. I just wanted him to be comfortable.

It was never the MS that drove me out. It was his need to take advantage of people and verbally abuse them and demean them. This was not my style and I just could not tolerate it much longer.

The Berkshire Express:
Down a Slippery Slope

AS HIS DISSATISFACTION with life and discomfort and frustration from pain became more prevalent, he insisted that if he could no longer make the trips to Hudson, New York for his cocaine, that he needed to use marijuana. Here we go again.

I kept in touch with my former lieutenant in the detective bureau at the police department where I had worked closely with him on the drug task force. I told him what was going on. He feared for me, my safety, and my son's safety. He insisted I had to get out. He was willing to come out and pack up my belongings and bring us home.

My life was coming apart. He was spending money uncontrollably, from the time we moved into the house he was buying new cars for each of us, paying cash, trading them back in a few months for something else. In three years we each had at least eight different cars. He was booking cruises that he knew he couldn't go on because of his health and then we would have to cancel.

And finally he sold a brand new Cadillac he had just purchased and bought an older model Audi, just because he wanted to look cool. He worked so hard at trying to relive what he once had that he wasn't paying attention to what good things he now had in his life. I tried to make his current life better in so many different ways, but it was never good enough.

At one point he told me that if he wasn't sick he never would have married me, I wasn't his type. He was used to girls like the Rockets and beautiful rich women. If that didn't make me feel completely worthless not much else could have.

I told him he needed to cut down on his spending or there would be nothing left for his care later on. He didn't want to hear it; he wanted to live for the moment. I had been there and I understood what he was doing, but it was going to only get him in trouble. He told me "Don't tell me what to do with MY money." It was not ours. He always reminded me that the house was HIS. The cars were HIS. He wanted to leave me with totally nothing. He once said he didn't have to provide for me because if he died I would just to back home and pick up my life where I left off. I believed that to an extent, and found that was not reality when I did return home.

The Berkshire Express:
Breaking Down

WE KNEW THAT Hawaii was the trip to end all trips. As time went on, occasionally Alan would mention maybe taking another cruise. I insisted that was not a good idea. Life was becoming more difficult for him. He was alienating himself from family and friends.

The holidays came and went. We celebrated my son's birthday, Christmas and Hanukah. I was becoming more and more unhappy. He was too. I just knew I had to get out, but I wasn't sure how I was going to do this.

The New Year arrived, 2004. I knew I had to make a plan for my escape. I felt so guilty thinking of leaving him. But it was coming down to him or me. I felt like I was losing myself more and more. I was a person of great faith and I prayed every day for an answer. On one hand I didn't think that God would want me to be wasting my life sitting on the bed with my husband watching TV, not talking, not seeing my family, and not being able to talk to them for long on the phone when I was able to sneak a call to them.

My son was miserable, I was miserable, Alan was miserable. I finally decided that as much as I wanted to make a go of this, fulfill my obligation, my marriage vows "for better or for worse, richer or poorer, in sickness and in health", I just couldn't do it. Life was too valuable and right now mine was slipping away more and more each day. I would become an old angry woman and I couldn't allow that to happen to me.

Alan's mental status was getting worse. I don't know if it was the drugs or the lesions on his brain from the MS, but he began telling me that his mother was there to visit him. He would tell me that he saw her car driving down the street and ask "Where is my mother?" I felt so bad for him. He loved her so much. When she passed away he took it very hard. She was his safe haven in the whole mess his life had turned into.

I listened patiently to him. Perhaps there was some truth to the story. Perhaps her spirit had visited him. I believed that he was so distraught over everything that she perhaps did come to comfort him, not in her car as the thought, but I believe when our loved ones pass they still watch over us. Maybe she was sitting on the edge of his bed as he described. I just knew I was not going to take that away from him.

Or maybe his time was coming close and she was there to "take him home."

The Berkshire Express:
Preparing the Trip Home

I KNEW THE situation was only going to get worse. I began to set a plan in place for my departure. It was not going to be easy I knew that. There was guilt for leaving. Uncertainty of what would happen once I returned home. Where I would live, work, etc.

I called a realtor that I knew. I had worked with her husband at the police station in my home town and she had sold my house for me. I told her I was coming back and needed to find a place. She found me a cute three room condo that was for sale.

One thing was out of the way.

I called the station and spoke with my former supervisor. I told her I was coming back. She arranged it for me, through the chief, to get my job back. Or I was supposed to anyway.

Two things now out of the way.

Slowly I made purchases of things I would need for my new life, my new home, household goods, etc. I would buy and bring them home and pack. I rented a storage unit and slowly took my furniture piece by piece, small things, boxes of things I had purchased; I would put them in my car while he was sleeping or in the shower and bring them to the storage unit. This went on for a few months.

His health was such at this point that we had people coming in a few hours a day, visiting nurses, etc., to help out. They couldn't believe how nasty he was to me and to them. I finally explained to them and the social worker that I just couldn't take it anymore. I was tired of being his beating board. They totally understood and were with me 100%. They helped me make all the arrangements for his care so that he would not be left alone. He would have someone come in to prepare his meals, clean, assist him with his meds, etc. Now I felt a little better about leaving. He would be cared for.

The day finally came. The rental truck was parked outside the door and Rick and I had begun to load it. I told him that I just couldn't stay anymore. I needed to go home. He understood. He was so sorry. He apologized for being sick. I told him it was not his fault and it was not the MS. That I could handle. It was everything else that I just couldn't deal with anymore; His drug use mostly and the nastiness. This was a job for someone much stronger than me and I couldn't do it anymore. I cried and told him I loved him and kissed him good-bye.

I was relieved, it had finally happened. I was out.

The Berkshire Express:
The Journey Home

WE DROVE TO my new condo and unpacked the truck. I was somewhat settled in and my son had to drive the truck back to the Berkshires to return it, as his car and belongings were still out there.

I thought he was coming back too, but he didn't. He stayed on for a few months living with my husband, my son being unsure what his next move would be. He had mixed feelings. He didn't want to leave his friends that he had made in the Berkshires. He had graduated from high school and was supposed to leave for college in Arizona. That actually was the deciding factor on me leaving. I couldn't bear the thought of being in that house with my husband and not my son. For eighteen years my son was my life and suddenly he was going to be out of it and I would be with this guy alone. I couldn't bare being without my son and my family.

My expected return to the P.D. didn't happen. I had been told that due to budget cuts the job was not available at this time. I ended up working temp jobs through an agency for about a year. They were very good jobs, one in the Vascular Surgery Department at a local teaching hospital. I had several other jobs with smaller companies for a few days or a week at a time. But the one I enjoyed most was with a very large well known insurance company. I worked there as a temp receptionist. It was supposed to become a permanent position and then the company was merging locations and a full time employee took the job instead.

I didn't know what was going to be next. Then I received a call from the P.D. the position was open and there were funds for it. I was to return to the station the next week. I was so elated. I thought finally my life was going to be back to what it once was. But we all know in reality, one can never "return" home. Things are never quite the same.

After I had been called back to my local police department to work full time, the morning after I had accepted that job, the insurance company called stating they wanted to hire me full time. I was so excited and suddenly realized that I had already made a commitment to the P.D. I explained that I had already accepted my former job back and how I was so disappointed that I hadn't heard from them sooner.

It has been five years now back at the P.D. Life is totally different there. I often wonder about those people at the insurance company and how things would have worked out had I taken that position instead. This is just one of life's unanswered questions.

I stayed at the P.D. and settled in to life sort of the way it used to be. Most of the police officers I had worked with previously had retired by now. There were so many new faces to remember. The clerical staff was the same with the exception of one. I was now on the bottom of the totem pole. I once was the shining star and now here I was just your average secretary. I once worked with the detective bureau, numerous government agencies, was privy to all the "secret" stuff. Not anymore. Life had completely changed. But at least I had a secure job and benefits.

Rick eventually returned to the area and stayed with me in my small condo for a couple of days and we both realized it wasn't going to work out it was just too small.

He moved in with his uncle where he already had a bedroom from his youth when he would stay overnight. His uncle took him in and he has been there ever since. He is now attending college and will graduate this spring. He has grown into quite a young man of whom I am very proud.

After returning and getting settled from time to time I would check in on Alan to see how he was. I guess in some small way I still cared about him, felt responsible for him. This one particular day I called and there was no answer. I kept calling every half hour or so thinking he might have been in the shower. Still there was no answer. I called all day and got no response. Now I became worried.

I called the neighbor across the street from him and asked if he had seen him around. He told me that he saw him get into his car earlier in the day and leave. I feared that he had gone out to pick up drugs. I continued to call during the late afternoon and still no answer.

The next day I called the local police to see if they had encountered him. They had not. I knew he did his cocaine buying in Hudson, New York. I called the Columbia County Sheriff's Office to see if there had been an accident of any type reported. I told them who I was and what was happening. They informed me that he had been stopped in New York driving erratically. They thought he was under the influence and found that the MS was actually the problem, as well as the drug.

They told me that they did not arrest him, but he had been

admitted to a hospital in the Hudson area. I was relieved that he was being taken care of and I felt he was where he needed to be. I inquired as to where his vehicle was located. They gave me the name of the garage and the address to where it had been towed.

I called the garage and they stated they did have the vehicle and how much it was to release it. I made arrangements to pick it up and told them I would be there the following afternoon.

I thought I had escaped the roller coaster ride, but here I was back on it again. What was I doing? He was not my responsibility any longer, to some degree anyway.

The following day I drove to his bank and got the money for the release of the car. My sister and her husband came with me. Someone had to drive one of the vehicles back to the house. We finally located the garage. If you've ever been to New York State, it is beautiful, but it is also very sparsely populated. We picked up the car and drove back to my place. I knew he would not have a license any longer. That was explained to me by the officer. He needed to sell the car before he got in serious trouble, with the drugs, driving and hurting himself, or worse, killing someone with the way he drove.

Rick and I have had quite a journey which has changed us both very much. I have a better understanding and respect for those with addiction. We are more aware of the needs of those with physical disabilities. In all, this journey has made me a better person and through all of the hardships, there were some very good times. I am thankful that I met Alan and we shared the experiences that we did. I think it changed both of us.

The Berkshire Express:
Retrospect

I KNEW AS time went on, that many of the faults in our relationship were also mine. I should have stood my ground as far as Alan making me sell my house. I was weak and he knew it.

I thought that I should have been more patient. I was very patient. Even his doctors would comment that they couldn't believe I put up with the things that I did.

I am willing to take responsibility for some of the things that went wrong. I knew what he was looking for in a wife and I wasn't willing to give up "myself" for that.

I know that many of the issues that Alan had were so deeply imbedded from his childhood that maybe there was no chance of repair, and topping it off with the effects the MS was taking on his brain, it was a constant battle for him.

The only family member of his that took notice of him was his beloved nephew. I was told that Alan would perk up every time he walked into the nursing home room. Alan was very proud of him.

While Alan was in the nursing home I was told he had gained a hundred pounds. I couldn't understand how they would let that happen. As far as I was concerned that was very poor care to him.

At the time of my divorce his lawyer told me that Alan "had a friend." She never elaborated on that, but I was happy for him that he had someone.

I received an e-mail the morning of July 5, 2009 from Greg's wife. He was Alan's health care proxy. She told me to "Call me immediately." I knew that wasn't good. I knew what to expect but didn't want to believe it. She told me that they had received a call from the nursing home at 4 a.m. telling them that Alan had asphyxiated during the night. Before the ambulance could get there he had passed away. Alan passed away in a nursing home, broke. The one fear he always expressed was that he didn't want to be poor. He once said to me "I wouldn't know how to be poor." Ironic that he drove himself right into that fear.

My heart sunk to the ground. I cried for him. I cried for us. I knew he was better off. He was so unhappy in the condition he was in. At one point during our marriage he asked me to help him die. I immediately said that I couldn't do that. Though I could understand why he would want that.

He once told me that he was happiest when he sleeps. That is when he dreams he is skiing down the slopes with the snow, wind, and sun on his face. He had once told me when we first met on line that he was a ski instructor and an assistant golf pro. Those were the two things that he loved most and missed the most.

Sleep in peace sweetheart. I hope you are skiing and golfing in heaven.

Light and Love my dear.

CPSIA information can be obtained at www.ICGtesting.com
Printed in the USA
BVOW02s1512080715

407399BV00001BA/51/P

9 781478 755623